Not Your Gran's Sewing Book

Not Your Gran's Sewing Book

Easy Alterations for the Perfect Fit at Any Size

Allie Luecke
Creator of Allie Upcycles

Page Street
Publishing Co.

Copyright © 2024 Allie Luecke

First published in 2024 by
Page Street Publishing Co.
27 Congress Street, Suite 1511
Salem, MA 01970
www.pagestreetpublishing.com

All rights reserved. No part of this book may be reproduced or used, in any form or by any means, electronic or mechanical, without prior permission in writing from the publisher.

Distributed by Macmillan, sales in Canada by The Canadian Manda Group.

28 27 26 25 24   1 2 3 4 5

ISBN-13: 979-8-890-03027-6
Library of Congress Control Number: 2023945027

Edited by Sadie Hofmeester
Cover and book design by Rosie Stewart for Page Street Publishing Co.
Photography by Kirra Jeram

Printed and bound in the United States of America

Page Street Publishing protects our planet by donating to nonprofits like The Trustees, which focuses on local land conservation.

DEDICATION
For my first sewing teacher, personal childhood seamstress, and forever cheerleader: my mom

Contents

8   What We're Doing Here

11 • Starting Strong
- 12   You've Got the Skill (Level)
- 14   Love It or Leave It: Sewing Tools
- 20   The (Fabric) Choice Is Yours
- 25   Meet Your Sewing Machine
- 32   Finishing Seams
- 35   Let 'Er Rip: Seam Ripping
- 40   Let's Get One Thing Straight
- 44   Hemming & Hawing
- 48   Get This Party Darted
- 53   The Real World: Dart Edition

61 • Under an Hour
- 63   Let It All Out
- 67   Take It All In
- 73   Let's Crop About It: Cropping T-Shirts

79 • Let's Get Waisted
- 81   Bring It In: Elasticating Waistbands
- 87   Around the Bend: Elasticating Tops
- 97   All Tied Up

107 • We're Busting Outta Here
- 109   Mind the (Button) Gap
- 113   Hips & Thighs Don't Lie
- 119   Zipper-ty-Doo-Dah
- 129   Grow a Pair of Pants

139 • Sleeves Please
- 141   Side Me Up: Shirt Gussets
- 149   Replacing C(r)ap Sleeves
- 155   Ruffling Feathers . . . and Sleeves

165 • Pick a Pocket or Two
- 167   The Outsider: External Pockets
- 175   The Inside Job: Seam Pockets

182   Glossary: Words You'll Actually Use

185   Acknowledgments

186   About the Author

187   Index

What We're Doing Here

Oh hey, fancy meeting you here in this sewing book I wrote. So, why are you here? Why am I here? Why are any of us here? Why **did** the chicken cross the road?

The simple answer: We are here to make our clothes fit better and have fun doing it, regardless of where you are in your sewing journey. (Unfortunately, my expertise does not extend to philosophy or traveling poultry.)

Maybe your mom taught you how to sew, but it was an indefinite number of years ago. Maybe nobody taught you how to sew. Maybe you learned how to sew in school but were too busy trying to navigate if your best friend hated you or not to retain anything. Regardless of how you got here, I'm so stoked to be part of your sewing journey.

I got into sewing as a kid. The very first garment I remember making was a blue camo fleece hoodie when I was around 11 (I had a huge camo phase as a kid). My next project was a pair of blue fleece pajama pants covered in frogs that were definitely too bulky to wear under my school uniform skirt in the winter, but I wore anyway. That same year, I sewed fleece winter hats to sell at our local craft fair to raise money to attend summer camp. Seriously, do we think I had enough fleece in middle school?

My mom taught me how to sew, and my grandma on my dad's side made incredible quilts for everyone in the family, so I was lucky to have good genetics on both sides. My mom taught me sewing basics before becoming my personal seamstress for every community theater production and school dance that followed. But as she will tell you, in adulthood I really took sewing and ran with it.

Some of you may know me from my Instagram account @allie.upcycles. On my account, I take old or thrifted clothes and give them a new life. I teach people how to make their clothes fit better while never taking anything too seriously. I also remain incredibly honest about the bits of sewing that can be boring or annoying.

I learned a lot of my more advanced sewing skills from watching online tutorials. Now hang on, don't go returning this book and jumping on YouTube! The internet is a fantastic free resource for sewing, but because it's free, we have to accept that beggars can't be choosers. Many online sewing tutorials are made by very lovely older women who, while they have an absolute wealth of knowledge, don't always deliver their lessons in the most engaging or relatable manner. I have loved sewing since I was a kid and want everyone else to love it (or at least learn it) too. It's such an invaluable life skill for people of every age that I want to make sure no one writes it off as a "grandma hobby."

Sewing has been cool on the internet for years now, so I'm not out here pretending I'm revolutionary in making it relatable for younger generations. But as much as I loved seeing my peers' creations and youthful spins on sewing, there was just one problem—none of these creators looked like me. Viral sewing videos of thin women with small chests taking baggy clothes and cutting off half the fabric to make something skintight are the norm.

But where were the people those baggy, oversized clothes normally fit? Where were the thrift-flippers who could barely find anything cute in their size in the thrift store to begin with, let alone something cute twice their size? Where were the people whose boobs took up an entire shirt while the viral videos were showing T-shirts transformed into cute little bikini-and-skirt combos?

Well, you know what they say: Be the change you want to see in the world. After years of hemming and hawing, I put my fears aside and made a sewing Instagram account sharing my very average U.S. size-10–14 body. I was terrified people would make fun of me, but instead, I turned out to be just what a lot of people were looking for (please know I'm squirming writing this as I try not to sound too full of myself). The thing I have been most grateful for with my sewing Instagram has been seeing comments and messages from people of all sizes telling me they're so excited to see someone who looks like them or that they're inspired to dust off their old sewing machine. The only thing I want is for everyone to feel like they can sew. That, and world peace.

I'm taking this sewing book in a different direction than other sewing how-tos. As with any hobby, I have found there can sometimes be a real air of superiority around sewing. I distinctly remember, early in my adult sewing career, reading an article titled something like "10 Ways Your Sewing Looks Amateur." The article was full of jabs about things I—and I'm sure many others—did as a beginner sewist that made my clothes look "frumpy" and "handmade."

There are SO many levels of sewing and so many different reasons a person needs to sew. Maybe you just need to know how to repair a pocket to save a pair of pants from the landfill. Maybe clothing stores don't carry dresses that fit your chest. Maybe, and I know this sounds wild in today's society, you just want to try a fun new hobby you may not be great at.

This book is for **everyone** who wants to sew. You don't need to be thin, you don't need to own all the finest sewing tools, and you don't need to be training for *Project Runway*. You just need to be someone who would love to make their clothes fit a bit better and have a laugh doing it.

x Allie

Starting Strong

Anytime someone learns I can sew, the first thing they say is, "I *wish* I could sew!" To that, I always respond, "You can! I'll teach you!" I'm still waiting on someone to take me up on that offer. That's where you come in, dear reader.

The growing popularity of sewing, upcycling, and thrift-flipping on social media is a double-edged sword. On one hand, it's incredible to be inspired by the countless people making or transforming their clothes and sharing the excitement of sewing with the world. On the other hand, incredible transformations shared only in an under-three-minute video can make people feel like sewing is complicated and unattainable. The reality is that you can make practically anything with a couple of stitch types and the right presser foot.

If those terms already feel far beyond your sewing knowledge, you're in luck! In this chapter, we're pulling back the curtain (which in my case is made of random swatches of scrap fabric) to demystify the art of sewing. I'll tell you the easiest types of fabric to work with as a beginner, teach you about the only stitches you'll ever need, and hold your hand through basic sewing principles. You will be on the receiving end of lots of new words and terms in this chapter, but have no fear! You can always find a quick definition in the glossary on page 182.

You've Got the Skill (Level)

Every project in this book has a recommended skill level: Beginner, Confident Beginner, Intermediate, and Advanced.

In this book, I'm assuming you're coming to me with an understanding of how to turn on, thread, and begin stitching on your sewing machine. If that is the extent of your sewing knowledge, that's absolutely fine! Honestly, I'm so proud of you for picking up this book and trying something new!

Even if you're new to sewing, I'm confident you will be able to complete all of these projects—yes, even the advanced one! I just recommend you build up your skills on the beginner projects before plunging into the more advanced ones. That said, I am not a good example of this—I always want to be challenged, and I always want to be great at things straightaway (which I assure you is in no way a problem and never leads to disappointment of any kind). To those of you readers like me, I salute you and wish you the best.

Here's what you can expect from each skill level in this book:

BEGINNER

These are the building blocks you will need to tackle any garment. We're focusing purely on the basics you will need to follow the rest of the tutorials in this book. Expect tips on measuring, creating and sewing straight lines, and all things seams.

CONFIDENT BEGINNER

Let's get into bigger projects! We'll start adding some elements like pockets (page 165) and gussets (page 141) to our clothes, but everything is going to be made of straight lines and stitches, so hopefully nothing should feel daunting.

INTERMEDIATE

Now we're cooking with gas! In these projects, we'll start adding bigger elements to our clothes, like sleeves. I'll introduce some more complex techniques like gathering (page 155) and facing (page 113). When I say complex, I really mean there's just more instructions that require more focus. There's also more math in these. Sorry.

ADVANCED

The big kahuna! There is only one project in the book I've classified as advanced, and it involves, dun dun *dun*, adding a zipper (page 119). This project will involve a lot of folding and turning of fabric, and it can take a decent bit of brainpower to comprehend. You'll still only use straight lines, but your stitching will need to be much more precise. But even if it isn't precise the first time, you can always seam rip and try again—there's no pressure here!

Love It or Leave It: Sewing Tools

A common misconception about sewing is that it's the cheap alternative to buying clothes. While you can absolutely learn to upcycle and thrift-flip clothing to make budget-friendly fashion, there are a fair few tools you need to make this happen. As with most things in life, there's a cheap way and an expensive way to sew, and I'm here to tell you the cheap way.

I am a saver, seldom a spender. I've put off buying items I've needed for *years* because the one day I saw it at the store, it was five dollars more than I'd budgeted for. While this can sometimes be a detriment to me, it's a real benefit to you. I will be completely honest with you about the sewing items you need and those you can survive without.

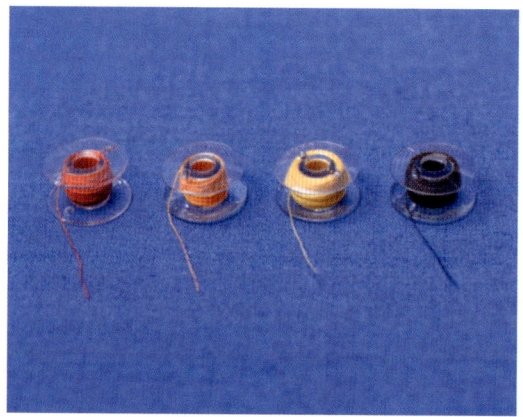

Bobbins baby, bobbins.

Bobbins

If you've seen any sewing content online, chances are you've seen one of the countless videos and memes depicting someone crying with the caption "When your bobbin runs out and you realize you've been sewing air for five minutes." Is the meme played out? A bit. Is it still accurate? Extremely.

A bobbin is a miniature spool of thread that lives in your machine, just below your needle. Every time the needle lowers inside your machine, a piece of thread from the bobbin loops around the top thread—the thread you've put through the eye of your sewing machine needle. The bobbin thread wrapping around the top thread is what holds everything in place.

The problem every sewist faces is that eventually, that mini spool of bobbin thread runs out, and if you don't notice in the moment, you will just keep sewing with absolutely nothing to hold your top thread in place. Before I start any project, I like to wind a few bobbins that are all the same color as the top thread I'm using. This way I can quickly reload whenever my bobbin runs out—otherwise I run the very real risk of giving up the project for, well, longer than I care to admit.

It's great to have as many bobbins as you have thread colors. That way you can always have a bobbin on hand that matches your thread. The important thing when purchasing bobbins is that you're buying the same brand and type that your machine requires (they should tell you in the manual). If your machine breaks from using a different brand of bobbin, it can nullify your sewing machine warranty. Rude, I know.

Bobbins come in both plastic and steel varieties. I've personally always used plastic and have never had a problem other than the occasional chip, but most things in my life are slightly broken, so I'm unbothered!

So how do you wind these bobbins? Each sewing machine is different, but they all create bobbins in a similar way. I'll break the process down for you, but you will also need to have your sewing machine manual handy.

STEP 1: PULL THE THREAD TAUT AND THREAD THE BOBBIN

Place your standard spool of thread on the long plastic or steel dowel on the top of your sewing machine (this is called the thread holder or spool pin, if you're feeling fancy). Pull the end of the thread and wrap it around the one or two small steel cylinders on the top of your machine. These are called bobbin tension guides, and your machine's manual will tell you exactly how you need to wrap the thread around them. Finally, you'll continue pulling the thread to the top right of your machine where a final steel dowel will be waiting for you. This is the bobbin winder, a.k.a. where you'll place your empty bobbin.

Identify one of the small holes on the top of your bobbin, then take the end of your top thread and thread it through the open hole, starting from the inside of the bobbin so your thread comes out the top of the hole. Once you've pulled the thread through the top of the bobbin about 2 inches (5 cm), place the bobbin on the bobbin winder.

STEP 2: WIND THE BOBBIN

Now the magic happens! You will likely need to push the dowel holding your bobbin to the right—this alerts your machine that it's bobbin-windin' time, not sewing time. Pinch the thread sticking out of the top of your bobbin between two fingers, then slowly press down on your sewing machine pedal. You'll see the thread from the standard spool start to wrap around the bobbin, like wrapping someone in toilet paper to turn them into a mummy.

Once you're confident the end of the thread won't slip out of the hole at the top of the bobbin, you can release the thread you were pinching. Now you can put the pedal to the metal and watch the thread start wrapping around your bobbin at breakneck speed.

I consider a bobbin full when there's about ⅛ inch (3 mm) between the edge of the wrapped thread and the edge of the bobbin. Once your bobbin is full, just snip the thread, push your bobbin and the dowel holding it to the left, and remove your bobbin. Now you're ready to slip it into its compartment under your sewing needle, making sure you're following your machine's instructions for which direction to insert it in, and get to sewing!

Chalk or Washable Marker

We're constantly tracing patterns, drawing seam allowances, or marking adjustments in sewing, so we need writing utensils. Of course, we don't want these marks to live on our clothes forever, so chalk or washable markers will be your best friends. Technically speaking, you could use pins for all your marking if you really want chalk or washable markers to be the hill you die on, but I promise your sewing life will be infinitely easier with a writing implement.

You can pay a pretty penny for specialty tailor's chalk or disappearing ink markers in a sewing store. Or you can stock up any time there's a sale on school supplies. For years I subsisted on a box of white teacher's chalk someone left out on the curb. As for washable markers, they've been making them for children for decades, and there's no reason you can't use them too. I personally prefer chalk to markers so I can just rub out lines that I've drawn incorrectly and avoid the fear of accidentally staining my clothes by ironing over marker and making it permanent.

If you are willing to spend a little more money, I highly recommend a Chaco Pen from Clover or Birch Creative. They're little pens filled with chalk that allow you to draw super-precise lines.

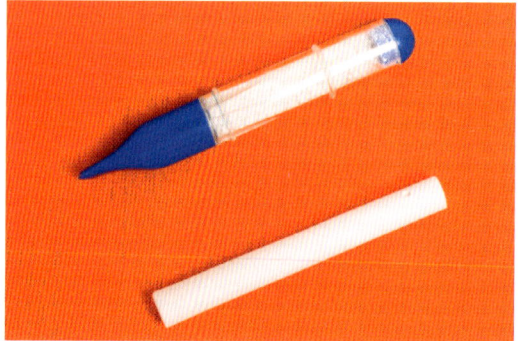

A Chaco Pen (above) and white teacher's chalk (below).

Iron

You have to have an iron, and chances are you already own one. Don't go out and buy a specialty iron just to alter your clothes. As long as the iron has multiple heat settings and the ability to turn the steam function on and off, you're golden.

Ironing Board

It is useful to have a proper ironing board but not a necessity. In place of an ironing board, grab a bath or beach towel, fold it over itself a few times, and place it on a table or on the floor. You can now iron garments or fabric on top of this towel. This is what my mom always does in winter when it's too cold to iron clothes downstairs in the basement with the ironing board.

Your towel should always be on a hard surface like a table or the floor. Never iron directly onto a surface; I know someone who cracked their kitchen counters doing this. You also should never iron directly onto your carpet, because you can melt the fibers. I've never done this, but it was a strict clause that my property manager really emphasized in one of my apartment rental contracts—he must have sensed my chaotic sewing tendencies.

Having an actual ironing board is most helpful when you want to iron one side of a garment without worrying you'll accidentally press creases into the other side simultaneously. It also serves as an extra table for all my unfinished projects. If you don't have the space to fit a full-sized ironing board, consider getting a cheap mini tabletop one to help you press your sleeves, collars, and any other cylindrical garments.

Measuring Tape

It's definitely worth buying this. You can usually find a cheap measuring tape in any drugstore. If you absolutely refuse to buy one but have some nonstretch string or yarn hanging around, you can use this as a makeshift measuring tape. Wrap the string around you like you would with a measuring tape and pinch the string where your measurement ends, then use a ruler to measure from the end of the string to the pinched place. Just make sure the string isn't stretching when you wrap it around you, or your measurement may be off.

Pins

No avoiding this one—you need to have pins. Without pins, you'll do hours of prep work with nothing to make your fabric stay in place. There are countless types of pins on the market, and honestly, the decision as to which ones you use ultimately lies with you. Each sewist has a very personal opinion on the best type of pins. I *love* fine stainless steel pins but constantly see online comments from other sewists bashing them. Weird, considering I thought I was the pinnacle of sewing knowledge.

Personally, I recommend having a set of long pins and a set of short. I love my long yellow glass head quilting pins (the ones my mom proudly called "the good pins" when she gave me a sewing kit for Christmas). These are a little under 2 inches (5 cm) long and work for practically everything. As I mentioned, I also love stainless steel pins with flat heads, measuring around 1 inch (2.5 cm) long. I find short pins are great for tighter or more delicate sewing.

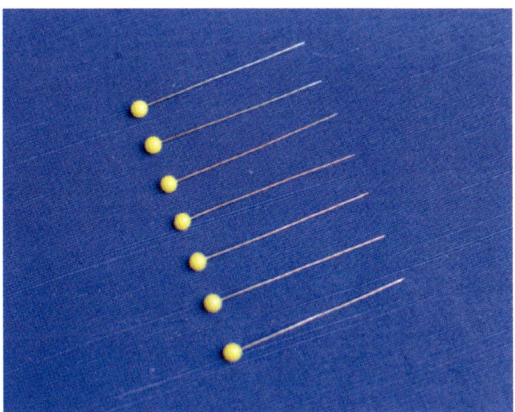

Long glass head pins.

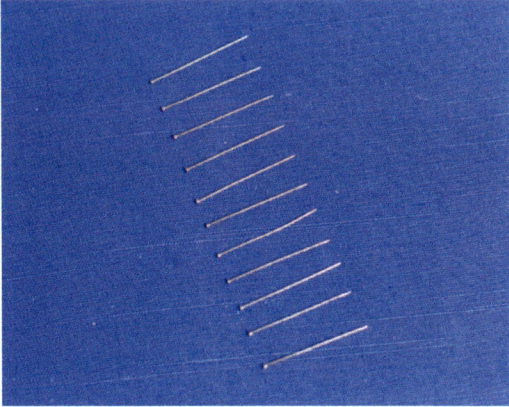

Flat head stainless steel pins.

There are two pin types I would avoid: flat flower head and plastic head. Flat flower head pins are great in theory. They lay completely flat, so your fabric isn't warped like it can be when you're using large round head pins. Unfortunately, I find the actual pin tips don't stab through fabric effectively. I thought I just got a bad batch in Australia, until months later, unprompted, my mom told me about the exact same experience she had with these pins in the United States. Scientific experiment concluded.

The other pins to avoid are plastic head pins. If you iron over one of these, you will be left with a Jackson Pollock–esque melted mess on your fabric and your iron.

Avoid these! *While excellent in theory, I've had bad luck with these flower head pins.*

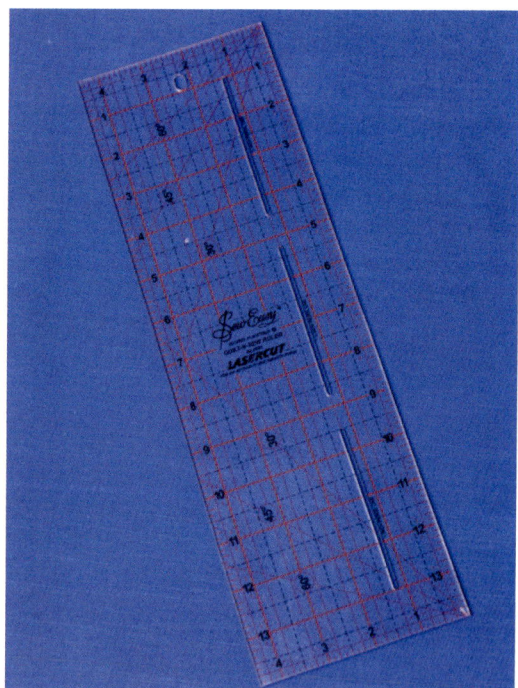

Quilting ruler.

Ruler

Sewing involves a lot of measuring, so apologies if you hate math. There are lots of specialty sewing rulers on the market, but you certainly don't need them. Until a couple years ago, I just used various rulers I found kicking around in drawers of old school supplies. That said, when I finally upgraded to a quilting ruler, I was beyond grateful I finally made the investment.

Quilting or patchwork rulers are much wider than school rulers, which makes it a heck of a lot easier to press down and hold your fabric in place while measuring, drawing, and cutting lines. These rulers are clear and have countless marks for different lengths and widths running every which way. This may make it sound like they are impossible to read, and admittedly you need to really focus sometimes, but the benefit is immense. All the markings make measuring and drawing seam allowances, hem lines, and any other measurements a breeze.

Seam Ripper

A seam ripper is perhaps the most important tool you can have in sewing. It's so important that most machines and sewing kits will come with one. Almost every single tutorial in this book will call for a seam ripper, and I assure you that virtually all your future sewing will too.

I'm a cheapskate, so I understand the desire to just use whatever scissors you have on hand to open a seam. I promise you it's not worth it. Seam rippers are a few dollars, and you can get them at craft or sewing stores, online, and at plenty of grocery stores or drugstores. Even the thinnest scissors, such as nail or embroidery scissors, are not thin enough to get through short stitch lengths.

Your trusty seam ripper. Get acquainted—you'll spend a lot of time together.

Any seam ripper is better than no seam ripper, but I'd caution against the compact ones that have a little cap. These ones just aren't as strong or comfortable to hold as the full-sized ones. I also recommend buying the brightest color seam ripper you can find because the only thing more frustrating than needing to seam rip is not being able to find your seam ripper.

Sewing Scissors

You're going to cut so much fabric in your sewing journey, and you need a decently sharp pair of scissors to do this. Sewing scissors can be shockingly expensive, but don't let this be the item that deters you from starting. If you can find a pair of large kitchen or paper scissors, you'll be able to get by when first starting out. You should definitely avoid using kids' scissors, though. Your hands will be absolutely miserable trying to get them through lots of fabric.

Learn from my mistakes and buy sewing scissors with plastic handles. Do not be lured in by pretty scissors with big gold handles—I promise they are much heavier than you expect, and your hand *will* hurt.

I recommend having two pairs of scissors, one large and one tiny. Tiny scissors are so useful when you're snipping thread because they're so much easier to control and get into tight spaces. You can buy embroidery scissors or just pick up a cheap pair of nail scissors at your local drugstore.

Sewing Machine

Any sewing machine will do. It doesn't matter if it's brand new, a hand-me-down from your aunt, or purchased for ten dollars at a thrift store. As long your machine turns on and off, has a straight and zigzag stitch, has adjustable stitch lengths, and can sew forward and in reverse, you can sew absolutely anything!

Thread

When you're first starting out with sewing, there can be a lot of start-up costs, and thread is one of them. As a self-proclaimed penny-pincher, I spent ages subsisting on black and white thread alone. As much as I tried to tell myself otherwise, this was a mistake. When you're new to sewing, a lot of your stitches will be a bit messy, a bit wavy, and really just a bit off. Which is absolutely fine and part of the fun of learning! If these wonky stitches are in a thread color that matches your fabric, people won't notice them unless their eyes are inches from your garment. But if your threads starkly contrast with your fabric, people can easily spot your mistakes (despite me pretending for years they couldn't).

You don't need to buy perfectly matching thread for every garment, but I suggest looking at your wardrobe, identifying the colors you wear the most, and buying a few spools of thread in your color palette. There are countless types of thread on the market for every specialty project, but just stick to sew-all polyester thread and you'll be fine.

The (Fabric) Choice Is Yours

I can't begin to tell you how many times I've chosen the wrong fabric for a project. Fabric shopping for me used to just mean "see something funky looking, buy it, and hope for the best." Okay, it was only because the fabric looked cool a few times—most of the time it was because it was the scrap fabric in the discount bin. Either way, I've ended up with a lot of fabric that I've realized too late will be a beast to sew or become a super-uncomfortable garment.

There are two kinds of fabric: woven and knit. Destined from birth to be mortal enemies. Or at the very least, destined to not work well together on group projects. So, what makes woven and knit fabrics so different?

If you loved visiting historical reenactment sites as a kid, you've probably seen someone working a loom, weaving threads back and forth across vertical lines of yarn. Aside from surely being the coolest kid in your school, you were witnessing the creation of woven fabric. Woven fabric is essentially a grid of threads created on a loom. This makes it extremely sturdy; easy to cut, fold, and sew straight; and not very stretchy or flexible.

If, instead of visiting Colonial Williamsburg, you spent your summers learning how to knit, you were probably the second coolest kid in school and know a thing or two about knit fabrics. Knit fabrics are made from looping one thread around another. This makes it soft,

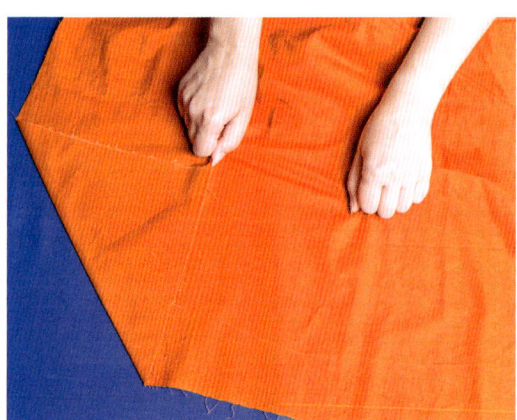

Woven fabric is not stretchy; it's easy to create a sharp crease by ironing; and the raw edges fray easily.

Knit fabric is stretchy and difficult to iron in place, and the raw edges curl inward but don't fray.

stretchy in all directions, easy to form to your curves, and difficult to keep in place while cutting, folding, or sewing.

If you were on a reality dating show, woven fabric would be the dependable guy you can always rely on, but you fear life with him would be too rigid and predictable. Knit fabric, on the other hand, is the adventurous guy who's stretching himself thin making bonds with every contestant, but he makes you feel good, and you like a challenge. Even though nine out of ten times I know you're going to walk away with the latter, I'm screaming at you through my TV to just pick the reliable one!

Common woven and knit fabrics you'll encounter in your clothes are:

WOVEN:
- denim
- linen
- gingham
- muslin
- silk
- satin
- twill
- drill
- corduroy
- flannel

KNIT:
- jersey
- lycra
- spandex
- mesh
- lace
- fleece
- crepe
- ponte
- scuba
- terry cloth

If you're new to sewing, I highly encourage you to work exclusively with woven fabrics. They will create a much easier environment for practicing all your new skills. Of course, you can't avoid knits—plenty of your clothes are made from them. Just know that you will need to be a lot more careful and calculated with your sewing when using knits. Any pulling or stretching of your fabric while you sew, even if you *swear* you weren't stretching it, can result in wavy, misshapen seams. I certainly don't want you to be afraid to work with knits! I just want you to have all the information up front.

Throughout the book, I'll offer suggested fabrics for each project. For every single project, it's a given that I suggest you use woven fabric.

Working with Knit Fabrics

If you are determined to work with knit fabrics, one, you're just as rebellious as me, and two, we'd better get you set up for success. The important tools to have on hand are a stretch needle, a walking foot, and patience.

A stretch needle is a sewing machine needle with a slightly rounded tip. This tip lets the needle sneak between the knit threads instead of stabbing and potentially snagging or ripping them. You can buy a five-pack of stretch needles for under ten dollars from any sewing store or website.

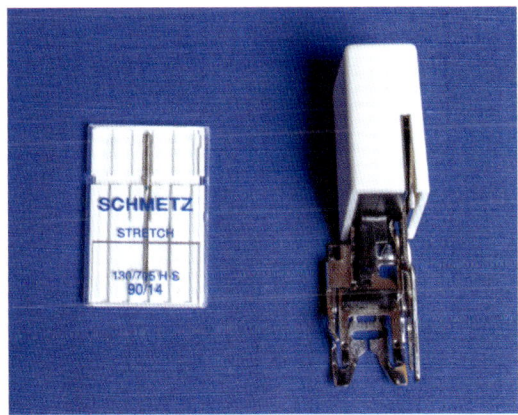

Your new best friends, you rebel: a stretch needle (left) and a walking foot (right).

I also recommend using a walking foot (don't worry, you'll learn more about this shortly on page 29). Knit fabrics easily pucker and become wavy as you sew them. Imagine that knits are a punching bag. The trainer, i.e., the presser foot, holds the punching bag in place while you, the needle, punch it and leave a dent. The way a standard presser foot holds knit fabrics allows the needle to push the fabric into the bottom of the machine, resulting in puckers and waves.

To remedy this, switch out your standard presser foot for a walking foot (see Presser Feet, page 29). The walking foot feeds your fabric more evenly through your machine without applying misplaced pressure.

Finally, sewing knit fabrics takes lots and lots of patience (something I lack). I'd love to tell you that you'll be great at sewing knits as soon as you try. I'd also love to tell you that the Earth isn't heating each year. But knits are tricky and global warming is real. (Luckily, you're helping to fight climate change by reworking instead of replacing your clothes!)

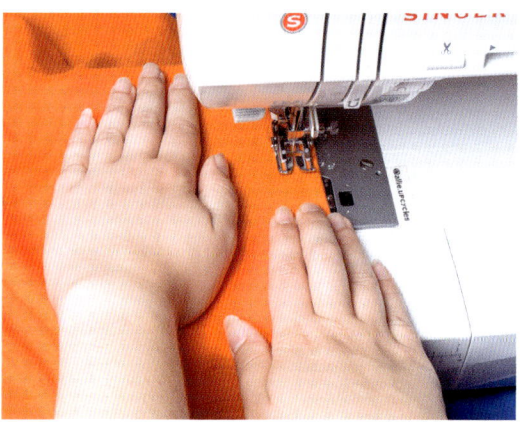

Keep things under control! Use your right hand to slowly push your fabric forward while using your left hand to stabilize and guide it as you sew.

Go slowly as you sew knit fabrics and use longer stitch lengths. Tugging or stretching the fabric as you sew is going to result in misshapen seams and a lot of cursing your machine. I like to lay my hands flat on my knit fabric as I sew, with my left hand directly to the left of the presser foot and my right hand a few inches in front of my presser foot. This allows me to slowly push the fabric forward with my right hand while stabilizing and guiding it with my left. Longer stitch lengths allow your fabric to stretch more after it's sewn. With stretchy knit fabrics, a short stitch length will cause puckering and prevent your clothes from stretching. For more information on stitch lengths, see page 25.

I hope this section either gives you the confidence to go forth and sew with knits, or the warning that you should really start by practicing on woven fabrics. Either way I'm coming out of here victorious!

Left: A knit fabric that has been tugged and stitched with too small a stitch length. Right: A knit fabric sewn to perfection (pats self on back) without stretching and with a longer stitch length.

I pretty much always use a medium-weight fusible interfacing like this one.

Interfacing

If you're working with any fabric—woven or knit—that needs to be sturdier, let me introduce you to your new best friend: interfacing. Interfacing is a special fabric you add to the wrong side (page 24) of your sewing fabric. It's used to make things like waistbands, cuffs, collars, and welted pockets stiffer and more pronounced. It can also be used on knits along seams and zippers to prevent them from stretching where they need to be structured.

Just like fabric, there are many versions of interfacing. For your everyday use, I suggest getting a nonwoven or woven interfacing that is medium weight and fusible. Fusible interfacing has a heat-activated glue on one side that allows you to iron it onto your fabric and save yourself the hassle of having to sew it on. Any fabric store should have multiple brands and types of interfacing available. Honestly, I just buy the cheapest one, and I've never had an issue!

Some interfacing comes with its own instructions for how to adhere it to your fabric, but if yours doesn't, use mine!

STEP 1: PLACE THE FUSIBLE INTERFACING ON YOUR FABRIC

Check which side of your interfacing has the heat-activated adhesive—this will be the shinier, coated side. Lay the adhesive face down on your fabric's wrong side. The wrong side of your fabric is the side that people won't see. For printed or patterned fabrics, this could be the uncoated or unpatterned side of the fabric. For solid-colored fabrics, you get to choose the right and wrong sides.

To keep both fabrics in place, you may want to stick a couple of flat head steel pins through the interfacing, fabric, and your ironing board so that the pinheads are flush with your fabric.

Place another piece of fabric on top of the interfacing—I usually use scraps from an old bedsheet or pillowcase. This additional layer of fabric will both help with the fusing process and prevent the interfacing from getting stuck to the iron.

STEP 2: IRON YOUR INTERFACING

Set your iron to the highest heat setting and turn off the steam function. Using the button on your iron that squirts water, spray a layer of water all over your scrap fabric. Now slowly iron the scrap fabric until it's dry (many instructions will say to just hold your iron in place for 15 seconds, but I'm always afraid this will burn a hole through the fabric, so I just iron super slowly). The steam created from ironing the damp scrap fabric helps melt the glue and fuse the fabrics together. Lift your scrap fabric to reveal that your interfacing is now magically glued to your fabric.

1

2A

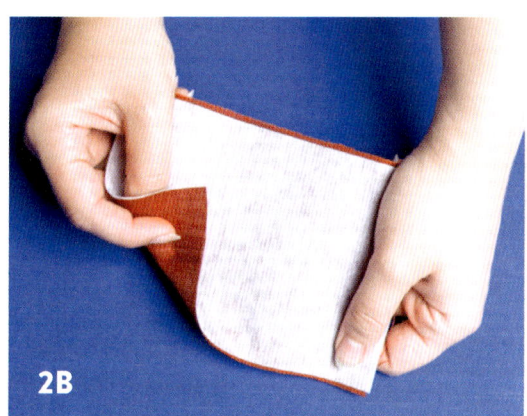

2B

Meet Your Sewing Machine

If you're brand-new to sewing, learning to sew can feel intimidating for one big reason: the large, foreign object with knobs and needles sitting in front of you. While a sewing machine may look intimidating, it's just here to make your life easier. Allow me to introduce you to your sewing machine and teach you the basics that will get you through any sewing project.

On any sewing machine you'll select two important things—stitch length and stitch type.

Stitch Length

Your stitch length refers to how long each stitch is, which is determined by how far your needle moves between each stitch. On a typical sewing machine, 0 is the shortest stitch length (so short your needle just stitches in the same place) and 4 or 5 is the longest stitch length.

Your stitch length determines how tightly or loosely your fabric will be held together. The shorter the stitch length, the stronger the hold. You may be thinking, "Well surely I'd only use short stitch lengths then," but long stitches have a place too! A great rule of thumb when selecting your stitch length is: the stretchier the fabric, the longer the stitch length. Your fabric can only stretch as far as each stitch length, so if you use a short stitch length, your garment can't stretch. It's like taking some delicious, stretchy mozzarella and cutting it to bits. Conversely, stiff fabric doesn't stretch, so you have the freedom to play with short or long stitch lengths. Long stitches are also perfect for basting or gathering fabric (we'll practice this in Ruffling Feathers . . . and Sleeves, page 155).

Throughout this book, I'll refer to short, medium, and long stitch lengths. When I say this, I mean:

Short: 0.5–2.5

Medium: 2.5–3.5

Long: 3.5–5

I live my life in a medium stitch length. I find a 2.5 stitch length is perfect for creating a secure stitch that I'm confident will hold my clothes together through thick and thin. At the same time, it's not so tight the fabric starts to pucker.

Stitch Types

The stitch type refers to the direction of your needle and the thread pattern it creates. The two stitch types you need to create absolutely anything are the straight stitch and the zigzag stitch. So no matter if you're using a machine with a handful or a wheelbarrow-full of stitch options, you can sew anything in this book.

STRAIGHT STITCH

A straight stitch is the almighty creator of the sewing world. Garments can't exist without straight stitches. Look at any garment you own and you'll see a straight stitch holding it all together (the same thing I try to make people believe I'm doing).

There are typically two straight stitches you can choose from on your machine—the only difference is the needle position. You can select a straight stitch where the needle is smack in the center of your presser foot or a straight stitch where the needle is positioned slightly to the left. Unless I say otherwise, assume I am always referring to a straight stitch with the needle centered.

ZIGZAG STITCH

A zigzag stitch is the second most important stitch on a sewing machine (always the bridesmaid, never the bride). It has two primary purposes: finishing seams and sewing elastic and stretchy fabrics.

When you use a zigzag stitch, your needle will move back and forth, left and right. If the needle is to the left, that's the zig, and if the needle is to the right, that's the zag. At least in my brain it is. These are not technical terms, but this is my book, so zig is left and zag is right.

From left to right: A short, medium, and long stitch length.

From left to right, zigzag stitches with: wide and medium length, narrow and medium length, and wide and short length.

On a standard sewing machine, you can adjust the length between your zigzag stitches, and on some machines, you can also adjust how wide or narrow the zigzag is.

Even when you're using a short stitch length, zigzag stitches don't have the same strength as straight stitches. If I'm using a zigzag stitch, I like to start and end by backstitching with a straight stitch before I switch to the zigzag stitch. This makes my looser zigzags less likely to unravel.

BACKSTITCHING

Almost every line of stitching you'll follow in this book begins and ends with backstitching. Backstitching is what locks our stitches into place. If you were hand stitching, you'd tie a knot at the beginning and end of each stitch line to secure it. But we have places to be and lives to live, so we won't be hand stitching here.

To backstitch, sew forward two to three stitches. Then hold down the reverse button on your sewing machine and sew two to three stitches backward, retracing the stitches you've just sewn. Now you can move on with your sewing and just continue sewing forward.

You should always backstitch at the beginning and end of your stitching unless you are basting, gathering, or sewing a dart. Kind of like "*i* before *e* except after *c*," but this time you're worried about your clothes falling apart instead of a spelling test. Honestly, I don't know which scares me more after relying on autocorrect for half my life.

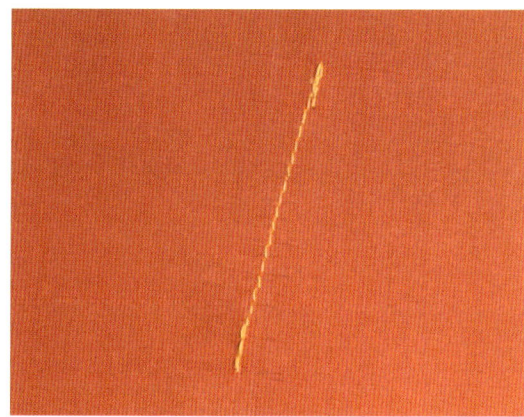

Backstitching at the beginning and end of a line of straight stitches.

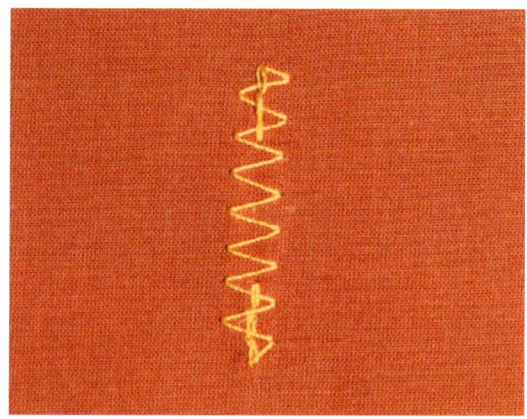

Backstitching with a straight stitch at the beginning and end of a zigzag stitch is optional, but I find it holds the stitching more securely than backstitching with a zigzag.

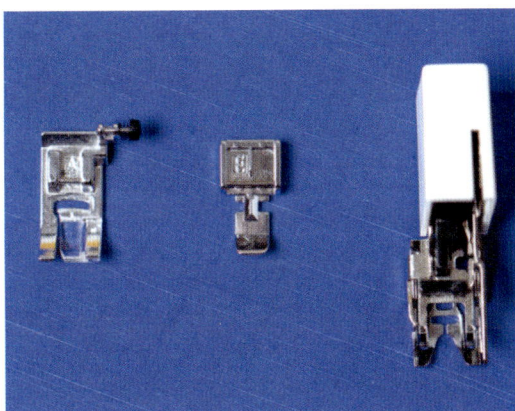
Left to right: Standard presser foot, zipper foot, and walking foot.

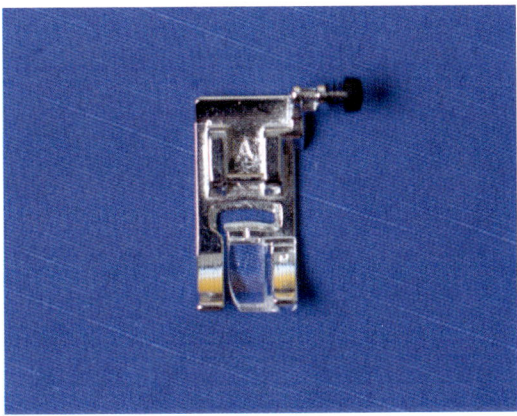
Standard presser foot.

Zipper foot.

Presser Feet

Look at where the needle is on your sewing machine. You see that flat silver thing attached below the needle? That's the presser foot. The presser foot is a 1-ish-inch (2.5-ish-cm) piece of metal that holds your fabric in place while you sew.

Your machine has a small lever that allows you to move the presser foot up or down. This is likely located either to the right of or directly behind your presser foot. When you're not sewing, your presser foot will be lifted, hovering above your machine's baseplate. When you're ready to begin sewing, place your fabric below the presser foot, press the lever down, and lower the presser foot so it holds your fabric in place. Whenever you finish sewing, simply lift the lever and raise that presser foot back up so you can remove your fabric.

Nowadays, it feels like there are as many different presser feet as there are mascaras in a drugstore. You of course have your standard foot but also your zipper foot, button foot, edgestitching foot, walking foot, blind hem foot, roller foot, and more. Sure, each does something slightly different, but at the end of the day, aren't they all serving the exact same purpose? Sort of. While all presser feet hold your fabric in place, their differences allow you to create different stitches.

There are two presser feet you'll need to make any garment in this book. First, there's the standard flat presser foot that comes attached to any machine. You can make countless garments armed with nothing but this foot. Your needle sits directly in the center of this foot, and the sides of the foot keep your garment flat as you perform straight and zigzag stitches.

The second most important presser foot, in my opinion, is the zipper foot. The zipper foot sits to the left or right of your needle, making it possible to sew *riiight* next to a zipper. This foot doesn't need to be exclusive to zippers, though! I use my zipper foot all the time to sew in hard-to-reach places.

CHANGING YOUR PRESSER FOOT

Changing a presser foot is simple but a little fiddly. Toward the back of each presser foot, you'll see a thin bar. On the steel bar hanging down from your machine, there will be a small lever that activates a latch with a tiny hook that holds on to this bar, like a claw machine grabbing a prize.

To remove the presser foot attached to your machine, press on the small lever, and watch the latch unceremoniously release the presser foot and drop it to the ground. Now to attach the new presser foot. While pressing that same lever down, put the new presser foot into position and release the lever. This should allow the hook to latch into place around the tiny bar on the new presser foot.

There is a third presser foot that should be in my rotation much more often than it is, but it's more annoying to change. You can call this the "nothing that's worth doing is easy" presser foot, more formally known as the walking foot. A walking foot is brilliant for sewing bulky fabric, like when you're attaching pockets, belt loops, or any other stacks of fabric.

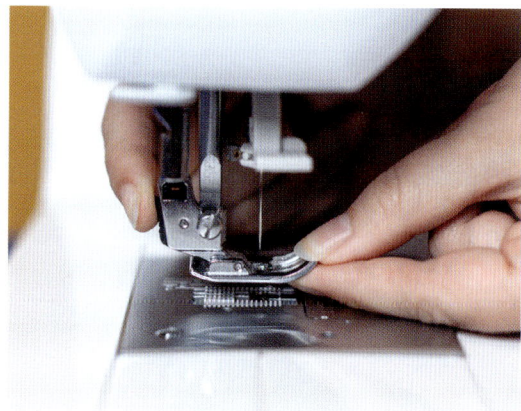

To change almost any presser foot, push the little button on the back of the presser foot holder to unlatch the old, then latch onto the new presser foot.

Walking foot.

To attach a walking foot, grab your screwdriver! Unscrew the presser foot holder, pop on the walking foot, and use the same screw to screw the walking foot in place.

A walking foot attached to a machine and ready to take on bulky fabrics and knits!

The walking foot is much larger than a standard presser foot because it contains a lot of mechanics. Typically it will come with your machine, packed in a separate box about 3 inches (8 cm) tall. Each machine and walking foot is different, so you'll need to read your machine's instructions (sorry, I hate doing that too) to learn exactly how to attach it. For any walking foot, though, expect to grab a screwdriver to remove the part of your machine that holds all your standard presser feet (hence why I put off using a walking foot until I absolutely must).

This meet-cute is now complete! I look forward to the complicated, beautiful love-hate relationship you and your sewing machine will have moving forward. Some days you'll work together as one perfect unit. Some days she'll make mistakes and you'll say things to her you don't mean. At the end of the day, remember you're both working toward one common goal: making you look incredible in your clothes.

Finishing Seams

If you're new to sewing, you don't know this yet, but finishing seams is going to occupy so much of your sewing time. I used to never finish seams because it totally interrupted my sewing groove. I just wanted to make things, not waste my time on mundane, trivial tasks! What was the worst that could happen if I didn't finish seams? Well, turns out, your garments fall apart.

Why do your garments fall apart? Chances are, at some point you've yanked a garment on or off and heard a thread snap. When you only have a single line of stitching holding everything together, there's no second line of defense once that snapped thread snowballs into an unraveled line of stitching. This is true for both woven and knit fabrics.

Woven fabrics, for all their positives, fall apart even more easily if you don't finish the seams. Any time you're cutting fabric to assemble a garment, you're creating a raw edge. Woven fabric is made by tightly weaving together lots of threads, so when you cut fabric, all the threads are now free to begin unraveling. If you sew a seam together but leave the edge raw, it can literally fray itself out of your stitching like a magician escaping handcuffs. And no one likes a cheeky magician. To remedy this, every raw edge must be finished with an overlocking or zigzag stitch, or else folded underneath and stitched in place.

A raw, unfinished seam allowance.

I don't want you to spend days sewing a garment only to have the seams fray and fall apart the first time you wash it (I may or may not have avoided ever washing certain me-made garments for this reason). Instead, use these simple methods to finish your seams and make your hard work last.

A seam finished with an overlocking stitch.

Overlocker/Serger

An overlocking stitch is a magical stitch that uses two to four separate threads to finish a seam in one fell swoop. If you look at any T-shirt in your closet (or on that chair that holds all your clothes), you'll see an overlocking stitch on the side seams.

To perform an overlocking stitch, you'll need a second machine separate from your sewing machine called either an overlocker or a serger. An overlocker/serger can sew two parallel lines of straight stitching while looping two different threads around the raw edge of fabric. It does all this while simultaneously trimming off your extra seam allowance. This machine is the greatest gift I ever gave myself.

That said, I'm a huge penny-pincher, so please know you don't need to buy one of these machines to make your own clothes. However, if you believe time is money, then spending a few hundred dollars on an overlocker is actually *saving* you thousands of dollars in time.

An overlocker/serger.

Zigzag Stitch

The zigzag stitch is the frugal person's overlocking stitch. The zigzag stitch is available on practically any standard sewing machine, which means you don't need to find extra cash or space to add an overlocker to your machine collection. You can achieve the exact same benefits of an overlocker with a zigzag stitch; it's just going to take more time.

STEP 1: SEW YOUR SEAM AND TRIM THE SEAM ALLOWANCE

Before you can finish a seam, you have to make one. A seam is created by sewing two pieces of fabric together, typically with a straight stitch. Most modern patterns will instruct you to sew ⅝ inch (1.6 cm) in from the raw edge of your fabric (I like to use ½ inch [1.3 cm] when making my own patterns because I'm defiant). This extra fabric on the edge is called your seam allowance.

Once you've sewn your seam, you can trim off some of the excess seam allowance. I recommend keeping your seam allowance to ⅜ inch (1 cm) wide.

STEP 2: ZIGZAG STITCH ALONG THE RAW EDGE

Now let's head back to our sewing machine to mimic the overlocking stitch. Select a medium-length zigzag stitch on your machine. If you have the option to select the width of the stitch, choose the wide option. The needle will move to the left and right with this stitch, and we want to begin with the needle positioned on the left. Your machine should do this for you when you select the zigzag stitch.

Place your seam allowance under your needle with the raw edge facing to the right. Begin sewing at the end of your seam, backstitching at the beginning (see page 28 for a reminder on backstitching). When your needle is on the left, it should stitch into the seam allowance. When your needle is on the right, it should stitch directly beside the raw edge of your fabric. That means we're truly just sewing air on the right side of the fabric. Sew the entire length of your seam allowance, and backstitch to finish things off.

All of the air stitches will result in your thread wrapping around the raw edges of the fabric and tucking them in like a loosely swaddled mummy.

Let 'Er Rip: Seam Ripping

There are only three guarantees in life as a sewist: death, taxes, and seam ripping. If you're new to sewing, you are probably living in ignorant bliss that the thing you'll soon be doing most is sewing. Unfortunately, you'll quickly learn that seam ripping is in fact the most prominent aspect of sewing, especially when you're altering clothes.

Seam ripping, as the name suggests, is when you rip out the threads of a seam to undo the stitching. This can be done for many reasons. If you're like me (and most sewists, even if they try to deny it), the most common reason is because you've made a mistake. For our purposes, we'll be seam ripping the parts of our clothes that don't suit us so we can fix them. For this book and all sewing ventures, seam ripping is a nonnegotiable skill.

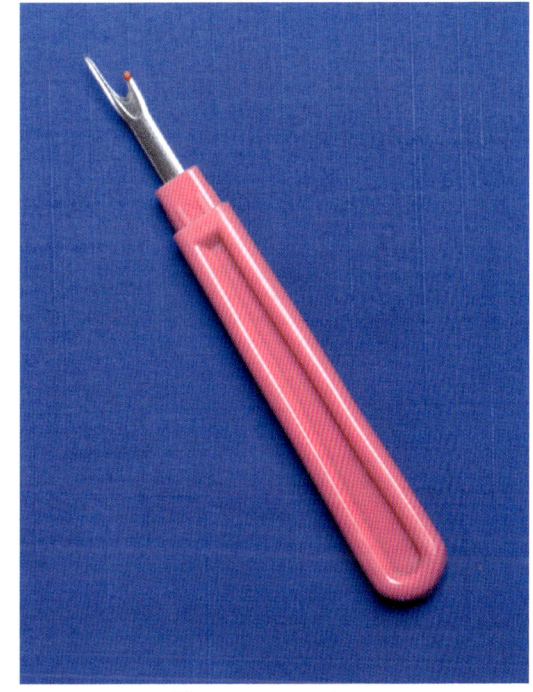

My trusty seam ripper.

STARTING STRONG

Choose Your Method

There are countless seam ripping methods, many of which I wish I'd known about way earlier in my sewing career. You can seam rip the outside or the inside of a seam. When I refer to seam ripping *the outside of the seam*, I mean ripping the threads that you can see. When I refer to seam ripping *the inside of the seam*, I mean putting your seam ripper between the two attached pieces of fabric and "blindly" ripping the threads.

OUTSIDE OF THE SEAM: EVERY FEW STITCHES

I prefer the outside-of-the-seam method for delicate fabric. It's a bit slower than other methods, but it allows you a lot more control and a much lower risk of accidentally ripping your fabric. If you're using this method to remove topstitching, like on a hem or a pocket, always turn your garment inside out and seam rip the thread from the inside of the garment. This is a precaution in case you accidentally pull or rip one of the woven/knit threads of your fabric—if it happens on the inside, it can just be our little secret.

On one side of your seam, slip the tip of your rip(per) under a single stitch. Either pull the ripper up or slide it forward quickly to rip the thread. Repeat this every four or so stitches along your entire seam.

Flip your fabric over so you can see the thread on the other side of the seam. The thread on this side will all still be intact. Using your fingers or the flat edge of your seam ripper, pull up on the center of the thread. As you pull, this thread will start pulling through all the pieces of ripped thread from the other side.

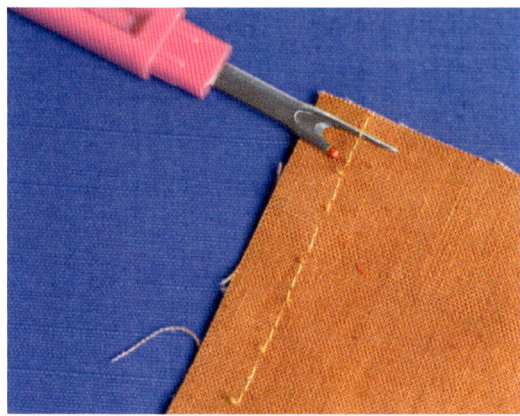

With your seam ripper, rip one stitch for every four or so stitches.

Flip your fabric over to reveal the other side of the stitching is still intact—magic! Pull the center of this thread and watch as all the ripped threads pull through your fabric and the seam is undone.

INSIDE OF THE SEAM: BALL INSIDE AND GLIDE

In my experience, the inside-the-seam method is the quickest seam ripping method. It can work on all fabric types, but I would avoid using it on delicate or super-stretchy fabrics. Not to scare you, but it's highly possible that you'll accidentally rip the fabric using this method if you're not careful (it's even more highly possible that I've done this a thousand times—learn from my mistakes).

We want the two pieces of fabric that are sewn together at this seam to be lying flat on top of each other. Starting at the end of the seam, carefully stick the pointed end of your ripper between the two pieces of fabric, under the first few stitches, and pull up to rip them open. We need to open the seam just enough to allow us to slip the ripper in between the two pieces of fabric and create a sandwich of fabric and seam ripper. The part of the seam ripper with the little ball on the end should be inside the seam, situated below the thread, and the sharp point of the seam ripper should be outside the seam, above the thread. We're going to slide our seam ripper through the seam, so if you have the sharp point inside, you run the very real risk of it becoming a jousting lance that rips open its opponent—the fabric—as you go.

Slowly guide your seam ripper along the inside of the seam. I like to lightly pinch this seam-ripper sandwich together as I go as a way of guiding the seam ripper. You'll feel invincible as the seam ripper mows through the threads with ease.

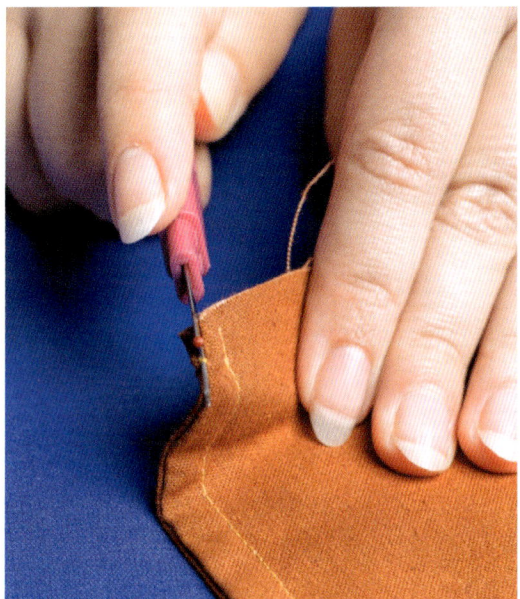

Stick the pointed end of your seam ripper between your two pieces of fabric and rip the first few threads of the seam.

Flip your seam ripper so the tip with the ball is inside the seam and the sharp point is outside the seam. Push the seam ripper forward and watch it mow through the stitches with ease.

This method can feel dangerously simple, so I implore you not to get too cocky and start pushing the seam ripper through at breakneck speed. It only takes one slightly stubborn thread to throw your seam ripper off course. If you reach any resistance, take a breath and pull out your seam ripper. Gently pull the two sides of the seam apart to see if that loosens the thread, and if that doesn't do the trick, use the sharp end of the seam ripper to rip a couple of threads. After this, you're good to reinsert the ball of the seam ripper and return to your regularly scheduled ripping.

OVERLOCKED STITCHES

If you're altering any store-bought clothes, there's an extremely high likelihood you'll need to rip open overlocked stitches. Because you're working with two to four threads, it can feel like the simplest plan of action is to attack any thread you can see with the seam ripper and hope the seam comes apart (unless that's just an ADHD thing and other people actually plan things before doing them). Luckily, you have me to tell you which threads to pull to bring this whole wall of thread tumbling down.

Each side of an overlocked seam will look different because of the way the different threads loop. On one side the looped threads look like teardrops or Os, and on the other side they look like Ys. On both sides you'll see a straight stitch running along the bottom of these shapes. Sometimes you'll also see a second straight stitch running through the middle of the shapes, though this is less common.

For overlocked seams, rip one stitch at the beginning and end of the bottom line of straight stitching.

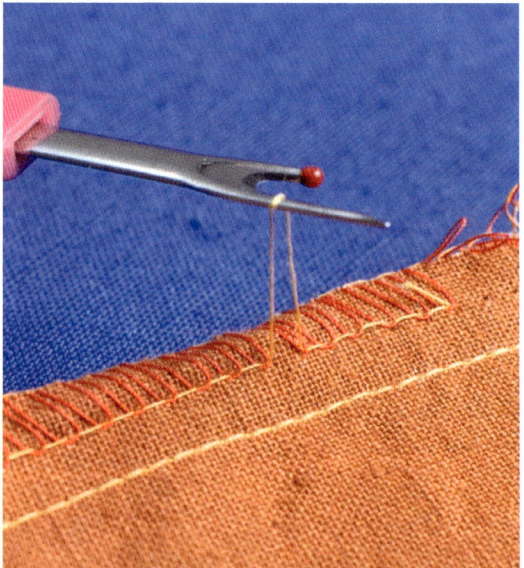

On one end of your seam, shuffle your seam ripper down a few stitches. Gently pull up on the thread until its tail comes loose from the teardrop-shaped threads.

Grab the tail of the loose straight-stitch thread and pull the entire thread loose.

Revel in the satisfaction of easily pulling away all the now-loose looping threads.

All our seam ripping is going to take place on the side of the seam with the teardrop/0-shaped loops. We're going to exclusively seam rip the straight stitch. It can be difficult to differentiate between the straight stitch and the bottom of the teardrop loop, like finding a needle in a haystack. The bit we're seam ripping is the stitch between two adjacent teardrops. Rip this stitch at the beginning and end of the seam you're ripping. Then, focusing on just one end of your seam, shuffle your seam ripper down a few teardrops. Instead of ripping this straight stitch, use your seam ripper to gently pull up on the thread until its tail comes loose.

Now grab this tail with your fingers and pull. You should be able to pull the entire straight-stitch thread out. If it gets stuck somewhere, seam rip the straight stitch at the point of tension and just repeat this process in smaller chunks along your seam. If you have a second line of straight stitching, replicate the process on this line.

Once your straight stitch is removed, it's time for what is hands down *the* most satisfying aspect of sewing—pulling out the looping thread. The looping thread has nothing anchoring it to your garment anymore, so give it one pull and watch this whole line of stitching unravel. It should release a similar chemical in your brain as when you peel an apple in one singular, spiraling strip.

You're now ready to conquer any seam that comes your way. Clothing is defenseless against you and your desire to alter it!

STARTING STRONG

Let's Get One Thing Straight

Do you, like me, struggle to draw a straight line even when using a ruler? Every time I think I've finally conquered the pen, I get too cocky and immediately knock my own hand to the side, and suddenly it's squiggle city. Well, I have good news and bad news. The good news is you're not alone! The bad news is it's me you're not alone with. Just kidding—the bad news is that sewing requires a lot of straight lines. But have no fear! I'll get you ready to create straight lines in your measuring, cutting, ironing, and stitching.

If you also had to use a ridiculously expensive graphing calculator in high school, you may remember a thing or two about creating a line. A line is when you connect any two dots in any plane of existence. You only need two dot points to make a line, but you need three or more dot points to confirm your line is heading in the correct direction. Okay, I feel your eyes glazing over; let's hurry up and relate math class back to the real world.

Marking a Straight Line

LEVEL
Beginner

SUGGESTED FABRIC
Anything you've got! You'll need to do this on pretty much anything you ever sew.

MATERIALS
Ruler

Chalk or washable marker

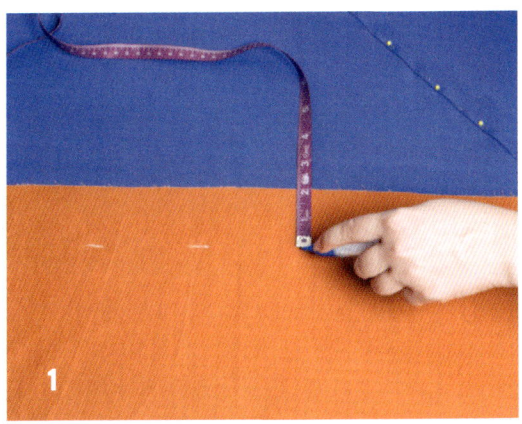

Step 1: Measure and Mark Multiple Points

Determine what part of your fabric or stitching your straight line needs to match up with. You might be creating a hem, sewing one row of stitching parallel to another, or cutting your fabric a specific distance away from another element.

For this example, imagine we need to create a straight line of stitching exactly 2 inches (5 cm) away from a raw edge. Line up the butt of your ruler with the raw edge and draw a mark at 2 inches (5 cm) using chalk or a marker.

Shimmy your ruler several inches further along, measure again, and mark 2 inches (5 cm). Continue this process until you've gone as far your new line needs to extend.

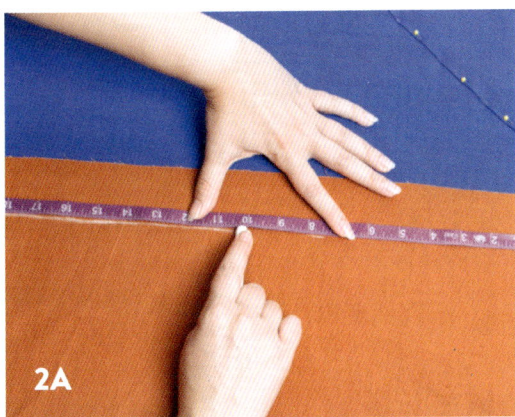

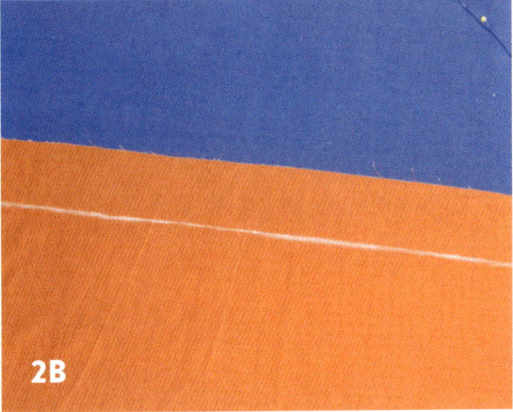

Step 2: Connect Your Marks with a Ruler

Line up your ruler with at least three marks at a time. If one of those three marks seems way out of line with the others, it probably is. That's why we made so many marks—to indicate when something seems a bit wonky! If a mark seems out of place, measure and mark again.

Trace along your ruler to connect all the marks. By the end, it should look like the world's lamest connect-the-dots drawing. But lame is A-OK because we now have a perfectly straight line that we can cut, stitch, hem, or iron along.

Ironing a Straight Edge

An extremely important note on pins: It is crucial that you use pins that have a flat, steel head or a glass head. Do not, I repeat, *do not* use pins with colorful heads made of plastic. You will end up with these colorful plastic bits melted onto your iron and fabric.

LEVEL
Beginner

SUGGESTED FABRIC
Anything you've got, though it will be way easier to practice this on woven fabric first.

MATERIALS
Ruler
Chalk or washable marker
Pins—steel or glass head
Iron

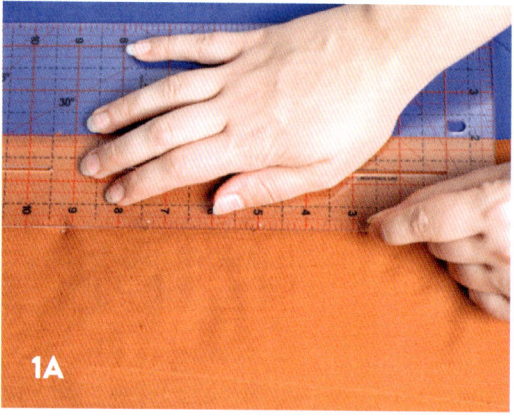

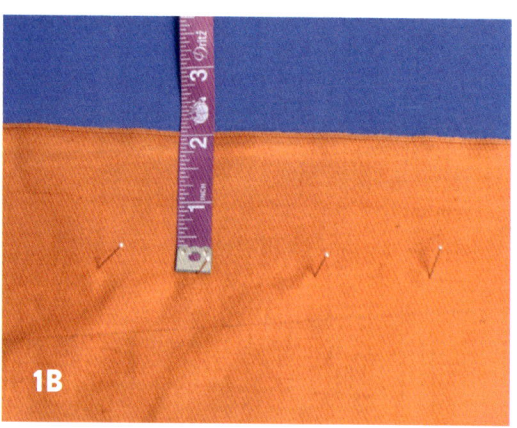

Step 1: Measure and Mark Multiple Points with Pins

First up, you need to know the width of the fabric you're going to fold over and iron in place (don't worry, we'll cover this in future tutorials like Hemming & Hawing, page 44). In this example, let's imagine we need to fold over 1-inch (2.5-cm) of fabric.

Lay your fabric right side down on an ironing board. If the fabric is slipping off your ironing board, place a chair or any random boxes behind your ironing board so the fabric can rest on it. Stop gravity from taking control!

Line up the butt of your ruler with the edge of your fabric. Measure and mark a dot that's twice the width of your future fold. In this example, that means we're measuring 2 inches (5 cm) in from the fabric's edge. We measure twice the width of our final fold because our fabric is currently unfolded, so once it's folded the measurement will be cut in half.

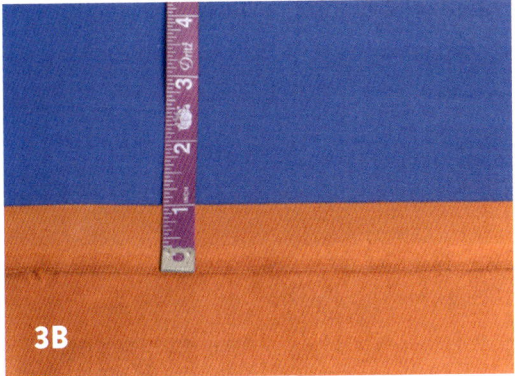

Take a sewing pin and stab it through your fabric and ironing board at the 2-inch (5-cm) mark. Shuffle a few inches down the fabric with your ruler and place another pin exactly 2 inches (5 cm) in from the fabric's edge. Continue with this until you've reached the extent of your ironing board.

Step 2: Fold Fabric to Pins

Grab the edge of the fabric directly below one of your pins and fold it up so the edge kisses the pin. Place a new pin just below this one, this time pinning through both layers of fabric and the ironing board. Once again, repeat this pinning process all the way down your fabric. Once you've pinned your fold in place, you don't need the old pin you were using as a guide, so feel free to pull those out as you go. You should now have a stunningly straight fold, ready to be pressed into place.

Step 3: Iron Your Fold in Place

Time to secure this fold! We have two options for protecting our irons from getting any scratches from the pins.

Option one: Push your pins all the way through your ironing board so the heads are flush with the board. Then take a piece of scrap fabric (I like to use an old bedsheet) and lay it on top of your pins and folded fabric. Iron the fold into place with confidence, knowing you've added a layer of protection between your iron and those scratchy pins.

Option two: Your pins can be pushed all the way through your board or still standing up straight. Iron only along the fold of the fabric, being careful not to reach the pins with your iron. Your fold will be held securely enough in place that you can then remove the pins and give a final official press across the entirety of the folded fabric.

Option three is to just not care if your iron gets scratched, but that's the chaotic gremlin in me speaking, and I'm trying to listen to her less.

Now you have a straight, crispy edge, and you're ready to take on any fold or hem!

STARTING STRONG

Hemming & Hawing

So, you're too short to wear pants off the rack without mopping up every bit of rainwater you walk past. Or that bandage dress you bought for homecoming a decade ago isn't exactly gliding over your luscious hips anymore, but you know you could chop off the bottom and rock it as a shirt. No matter who you are, you will need your clothes hemmed at some point in your life. You could pay the cost of this book to get a single pair of pants hemmed at the alterations shop in the airport, or you could just spend a bit of your afternoon hanging out with an iron, a ruler, and some pins. You will, however, need to get your Toblerone® fix elsewhere.

LEVEL
Beginner

SUGGESTED FABRIC
If you're new to sewing, choose a garment made with sturdy fabric, like dress pants or a woven cotton dress. Hemming stretchy knit garments like T-shirts takes some practice to avoid getting a wavy hemline.

MATERIALS
Garment that needs shortening

Pins

Chalk or washable marker (optional)

Ruler

Scissors

Iron

Thread

Sewing Machine

> **Heads-up:** Your garment will be inside out during this entire process, even when you're trying it on.

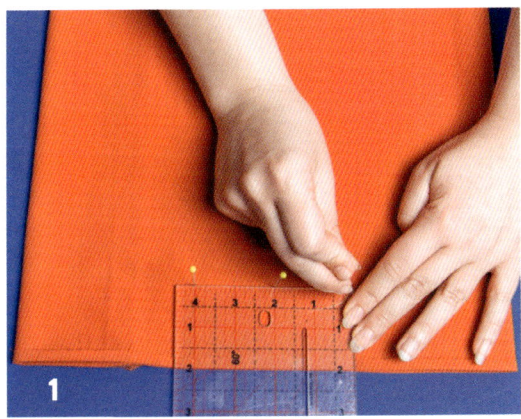

Step 1: Mark Your New Length and Choose Your Hem Width

We start by making two non-life-altering decisions: Where do you want the new hem of your garment, and how wide do you want said hem to be?

If you're hemming pants or long skirts and dresses, make sure to try them on with the typical shoes you'd wear with them. If you're hemming a shirt, put on bottoms that are the rise you typically wear. When deciding on the length of your shirt hem, you should love the length when it's untucked, but also make sure it will still be long enough to stay tucked in if you don't want to exist solely in crop tops. Like Sisyphus with his boulder, I have condemned myself to a life of retucking shirts I hemmed *juuust* too short, so please, do as I say, not as I do.

Once you've decided where you want your garment to end, mark this spot with a pin, chalk, or washable marker.

As for the width of the hem, I'd say the sky's the limit, but your fate is determined by how much fabric you have to work with. Fabric permitting, you can do anything from a micro-hem to a 7-inch (18-cm) hem if that's your vibe. A micro-hem is typically used for flowy silk and satin garments or sheer fabric and is more advanced (read: annoying to feed through your sewing machine). A wide hem is best suited to boxy tops and dresses or wide-legged pants as it helps create balance. For most projects, especially when you're first starting out, a ½- to 1-inch (1.3- to 2.5-cm) hem will work perfectly—it's simple to measure, easy to feed through your sewing machine, and mimics the hem of most of your clothes.

Step 2: Cut Off Excess Fabric

Now let's cut off any excess fabric. How much fabric can you cut off while still having enough fabric for the hem? To answer that, we need to do the simplest bit of math:

Desired width of hem + ¼ inch (6.5 mm)

For example, if you want a 1-inch (2.5-cm) hem, measure 1¼ inches (3.2 cm) below your new hem mark, and cut off any excess fabric below that. If you want tips on cutting a straight line, head on back to Let's Get One Thing Straight (page 40).

Step 3: Iron Your New Hem

To the ironing board! We're going to do two bits of ironing to prepare the hem for sewing, which if you had asked me at age 21 would have been three too many times to be forced to iron.

With your garment inside out, take the bottom ¼ inch (6.5 mm) of fabric, fold it up, and iron it flat into place. Now, chances are you can't fold and iron the entirety of the hem all at once. Just fold your fabric up, iron the length of the fabric that fits on your ironing board, then shuffle the fabric along and repeat. Fold, iron, shuffle, fold, iron, shuffle, and so on until you get back to where you started.

Now for that second bit of ironing I promised you. With the bottom ¼ inch (6.5 mm) of fabric still folded up, fold the new bottom of your fabric up. If you want a 1-inch (2.5-cm) hem, fold up 1 inch (2.5 cm) of fabric. A 2-inch (5-cm) hem, 2 inches (5 cm) of fabric. You get the idea. Iron this fold into place.

Because we folded up ¼ inch (6.5 mm) of fabric and then folded our fabric again, the raw edge of the fabric is now fully enclosed.

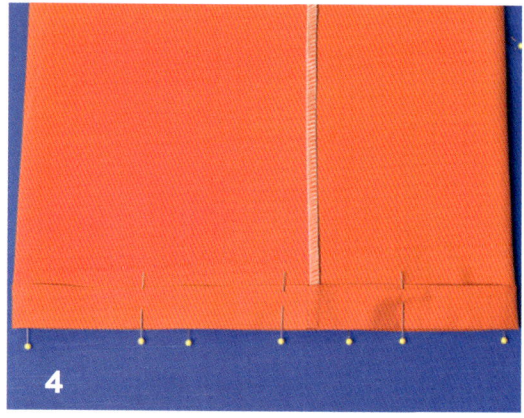

Step 4: Pin Your Hem in Place

We are just minutes away from sewing this bad boy! The last bit of prep work is to pin your hem in place. Even though we've ironed everything into position, we want to reinforce these folds by placing a pin every few inches along the hem. This will prevent our fabric from shifting out of place while we sew. Think of it like JELL-O®. The ironing is the gelatin and the pins are the mold. When you take JELL-O out of a mold, the gelatin holds the JELL-O's shape, but without the mold, the shapely JELL-O is free to wiggle about. And sewing JELL-O is hard.

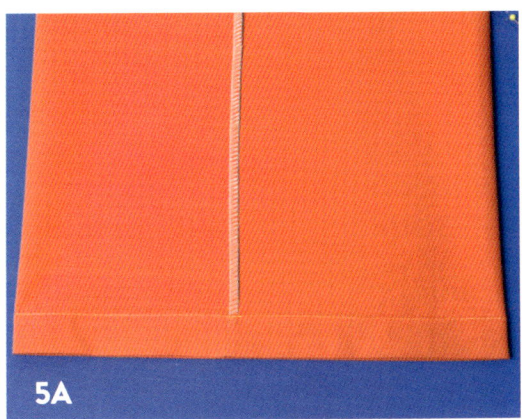
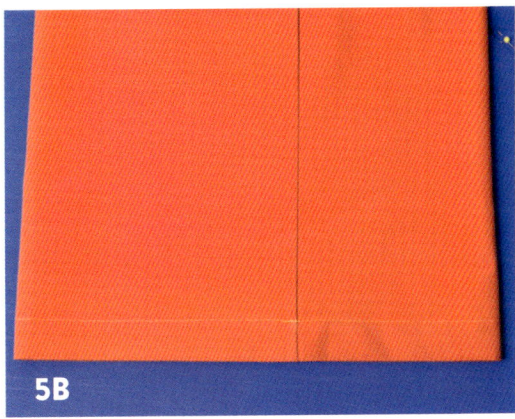

Step 5: Sew Your Hem

To the sewing machine, Batman!

If you're sewing a pant hem, the bottom of the pants may be too small to fit around your sewing machine, but don't worry, sewing machine manufacturers have accounted for this! The front few inches of a modern sewing machine base should be detachable, so you can just slide it right off and hopefully fit your small textile cylinder. I say hopefully because there are skinny jeans in this world too skinny for any machine.

Now let's set our stitch type and length. Select a straight stitch and choose a medium–long stitch length. I personally always select a 3 to 3.5 stitch length for hems. This stitch is going to be fully visible on the outside of your garment, and honestly a longer stitch length just looks way nicer and neater. We also don't need a super-short, tight stitch because this isn't a seam that's going to receive a lot of strain (like every chest seam on my shirts); we're just holding some folded fabric in place.

Now. Finally. Let's sew! We're going to edgestitch this hem into place, meaning we're going to stitch as close as we can to the top of the hem. If I'm hemming pants or shorts, I like to begin sewing several stitch lengths in front of the inseam (the seam between your legs). This is because we need to backstitch (page 28) at the beginning and end of our hem. Sometimes this makes the thread more noticeable, so I try to keep it as hidden as possible. Keep sewing all the way around your hem until you're right back where you started. Backstitch again at the end to pop and lock that thread into place.

As you're sewing, go as *slooowly* as you need. Because this is such a visible stitch, we really want to ensure the stitching is as straight and neat as possible. Sewing fast may feel great in the moment, but talk to me after you realize the stitching is super wonky and you have to seam rip it all out and do it all over again. As someone who's done this a thousand times, I can confirm the need for speed is never worth it.

Step 6: Iron Once More with Feeling

With the stitching done, there's just one step left that's so small it's only one sentence: Iron the hem one last time to make it extra crisp.

Now give yourself a pat on the back and go enjoy your perfectly hemmed garment!

Get This Party Darted

Have you ever had gaping clothes? Maybe the waist of your pants always sits an inch away from your body. Or your tank tops always leave a weird peekaboo to your bra. If gaping is the problem, darts are the solution. Darts take a piece of flat, 2-D fabric and transform it into a 3-D garment designed to perfectly shape to your curves. If you're unfamiliar with darts as a sewing term and have instead believed this whole time I was talking about darts you throw at a board in a bar, things can only make more sense from here.

Darts are pivotal to making your clothing fit better, so there's no one place for this tutorial to live. As well as being everywhere, darts are deceptively difficult to master. Sewing a straight line is about as basic as you can get, but even though a dart is essentially just a straight line, there's a lot more to it than meets the eye.

In this tutorial, I'll walk you through the basics of creating a dart on a flat surface. I encourage you to follow along and practice this a few times on a piece of scrap fabric before adding darts to your clothes. That said, if your brain is wired like mine and demands more dopamine at every second, I won't hold it against you if you skip the practice and dive headfirst into the real thing.

In that case, you may want to flip to The Real World: Dart Edition (page 53).

LEVEL
Beginner

SUGGESTED FABRIC
Use a stiff woven fabric to practice. It should be around 4 x 8 inches (10 x 20 cm) minimum.

MATERIALS
Scrap fabric

Iron

Ruler

Chalk or washable marker

Pins

Thread

Sewing machine

> **Heads-up:** The measurements we're using for this dart are just to make practicing easy. Your darts will vary in width and length depending on your garments and body.

Step 1: Measure and Mark Your Dart

Take a flat piece of fabric and fold it in half with the right sides touching. Grab your iron and press the fold flat. When you're using this method on a garment, you'll press the fold only where your dart will go, but it will make the whole practice process easier to have everything pressed flat.

Line up the butt of your ruler with the folded edge and the measuring side of your ruler with the raw edge at the top of your fabric. Measure ¾ inch (1.9 cm) in from the fold and mark it with chalk or a marker. Now line up the measuring side of your ruler with the fold, measure 5 inches (13 cm) down from the top raw edge, and make another mark. Using chalk or a marker, draw a straight line to connect your two marks.

You have two options for pinning your dart to make it sewing machine–ready. You can place pins perpendicular to your folded edge, ensuring the final pin lines up exactly with the tip of your dart, also called the dart point. Alternatively, you can trace the line we just drew, also called the dart leg, by placing your pins along the line. The points of your pins should be facing the fabric's top raw edge. With this method, you should still place a final pin perpendicular to the fold at the dart point. This is the method I've used in this example.

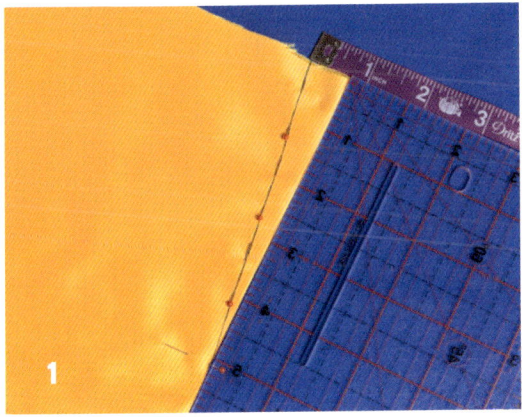

Step 2: Sew Your Dart

Let's sew this dart (if you prefer playing darts, you're welcome to grab a beer and stand on a sticky floor while you sew to give yourself a similar experience). Set your sewing machine to a short–medium length straight stitch. Place your fabric on your machine so that the fold is on the right side of your presser foot and the top raw edge is at, well, the top.

When sewing a dart, you *always* start stitching from the top of the fabric, never from the dart point. I learned this after starting many a dart from the dart point and ending up with a knotted, puckered mess. Backstitch at the top of the dart and then continue sewing along the line you've drawn or pinned. Regardless of the way in which you've pinned your dart, make sure you remove the pins as you go *before* you sew over them.

As your stitching nears the dart point (about 1 inch [2.5 cm] away), approach the line the same way my hometown approaches speed limits: merely as a guide, not as a rule. Instead of sewing the end of the line perfectly straight, we're going to stitch it at a slight curve. This is going to make the dart better suited for fitting our bodies, since we have curves instead of sharp angles. Very gently pull your fabric toward the left as you continue sewing straight. Your stitching will curve slightly as your needle creeps closer and closer to the fold of your fabric.

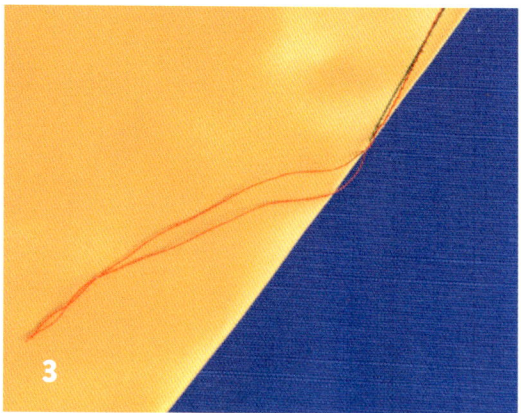

Step 3: Tie Off Your Dart

Now place your needle in the up position, lift your presser foot, and pull your fabric away from the machine until you've pulled out a bobbin-thread and top-thread tail of about 4 inches (10 cm) each. Snip your thread at the machine, keeping your garment's tail long.

When you reach the edge of your fold, continue sewing a few more stitches until your needle is no longer sewing through your fabric but is instead stitching the air to the right of your fold. Your needle should be just grazing the fabric with the final stitches, catching mere fibers until there's nothing left to catch, and it looks as if your stitches have melted off the folded edge. Do *not* cut your thread yet.

Tie the top and bobbin thread into a simple, tight double knot at the dart point. Snip your remaining thread tails to about ½ inch (1.3 cm) long. The tail just needs to be long enough that your knot isn't at risk of unraveling (like me when I'm trying to remember where I put my phone when I'm already three minutes late leaving for my train).

Step 4: Press Your Dart

Finally, we need to iron our dart. Unfold your fabric, lay your dart on one side of the seam, and iron it flat along the seam, stopping an inch (2.5 cm) above the dart point.

Because our fabric is now 3-D, the dart point will be curved, meaning we can't just iron it flat the way we would a standard seam. When pressing a dart, you're supposed to use a tailor's ham to press the curve. A tailor's ham is a small rectangular pillow with completely curved edges and corners. The ham functions as a curved ironing board to help create the perfect shape in your dart.

I do not own a tailor's ham. It's one of those things that looks super easy to make, so I've never bought one, but then I have also never gotten around to making one. Instead, to press the tip of my dart, I bring it to the very edge of my ironing board where the board curves slightly and press along that edge.

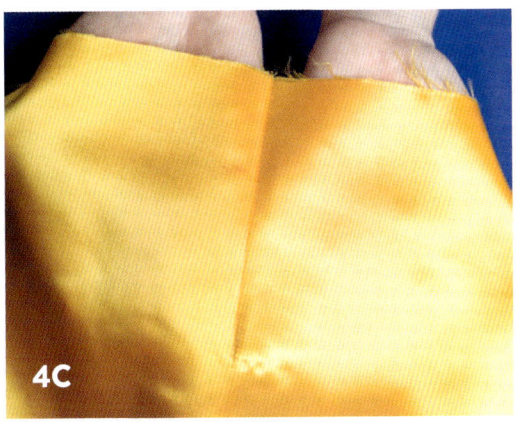

You can also ball up a plain T-shirt and place it under your dart as a makeshift tailor's ham. Just make sure there are no screen-printed graphics on the T-shirt—you don't want to melt the graphics onto your dart and ruin two garments at once. Or maybe you do; who am I to deny you your destructive tendencies?

When your dart is properly sewn and pressed, it will just blend into the rest of the fabric with the dart point practically indiscernible from the fabric below it. The dart will just blend into the rest of your fabric. If your dart doesn't look like this, please don't fret! Sewing darts sounds like it should be so simple, but the reality is that it takes a lot of practice to get a perfect dart point.

Troubleshooting

If your dart point ends in a little divot or dimple once it's pressed, there are a couple ways you can try to remedy this. The first is to continue pressing it—once more with feeling! You may need to gently pull apart the fabric on both sides of the dart to make sure it is as smooth as possible while you continue pressing on a curved surface.

If the dimple still doesn't disappear, you may need to resew the dart. You may have sewn at too sharp of an angle when approaching the folded edge. In this case you'll need to ensure you're gradually creating a more curved line as you approach the fold. Alternatively, you may not have sewn all the way to the very edge of the fold, in which case you'll need to ensure you're sewing past the fold of your garment, stitching nothing but air at the end.

I have complete faith that with practice, you'll master this! And if you don't quite master it and your dart still has a dimple, guess what? You can still wear it because dimples are adorable.

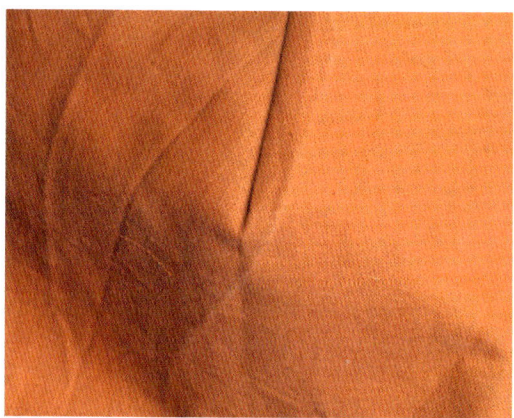

A dart dimple.

A dart sewn at too sharp an angle.

A dart where the stitching doesn't extend far enough to the edge.

The Real World: Dart Edition

Now let's find out what happens when we stop practicing darts on scrap fabric and start getting real. Time to gather your garments that need darts!

Darts can be added virtually anywhere you need to fit a garment around your curves. The key places you'll use them on a dress or shirt will be at the bust and waist, and the key places you'll use them on a skirt, shorts, or pants will be around the waist.

LEVEL
Confident Beginner

SUGGESTED FABRIC
A top where the armhole is gaping or bottoms with a loose waistband.

MATERIALS
Gaping garment
Pins
Ruler
Chalk or washable marker
Thread
Sewing machine
Iron

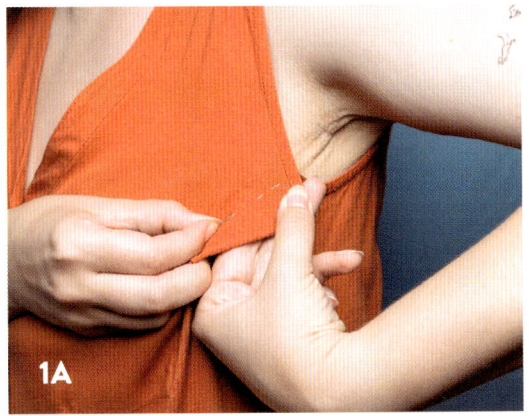
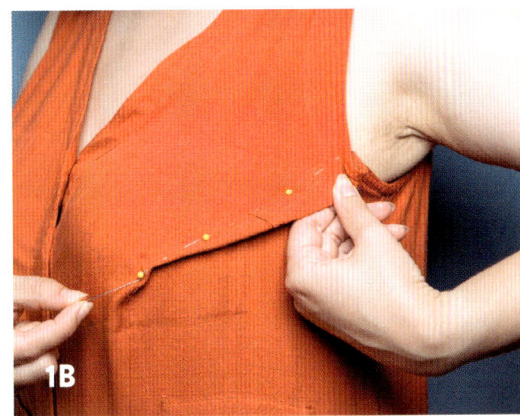
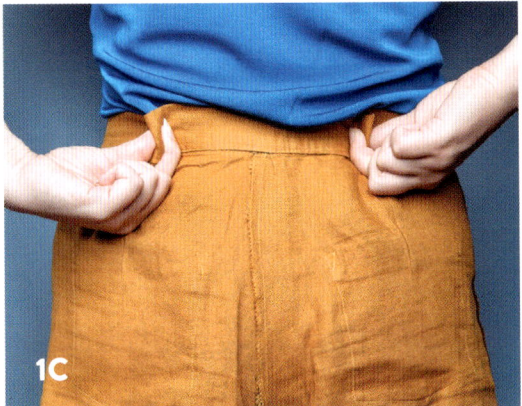
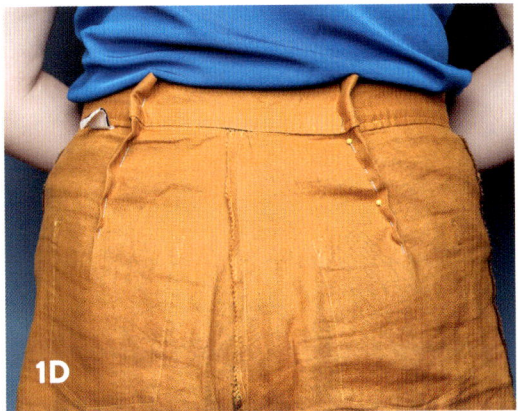

Step 1: Try On Your Garment and Pin Your Darts

Try on your gaping clothes inside out. You should be able to easily see where your clothes are sticking out from your body. If you're adding darts to armhole openings, you'll pinch the fabric so that the top of the dart lines up with your armpit fat. See, armpit fat isn't entirely useless—it officially has one single purpose. If you're adding darts to the waistband on pants, your darts should line up roughly with the center of each back pocket (or where pockets would be if you're forced to play make believe).

Along the top of this opening, use your fingers to pinch the gaping fabric and pin it together. Your pin should be flat against your body, creating the first part of your dart leg.

Continuing along the same line, keep pinching and pinning your fabric together until you reach the point where your garment naturally sits flush on your body. Make sure the head of your final pin is exactly where the dart naturally ends. Repeat this process on the opposite side of your garment.

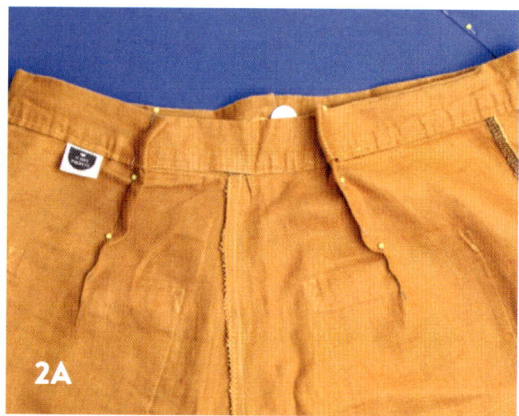

Step 2: Fix Up and Sew Your Darts

Pinning a garment on your own body is always going to be a bit tricky and end up a little bit wonky. So, let's fix up these darts.

Ever so gently take off your garment. It's crucial you don't dislodge these pins and preferable that you don't prick yourself with them. But in my experience, you haven't finished a garment until you've yelled an expletive at a pin that's just stabbed you.

Lay down your inside-out garment. Make sure that where the very top of your dart is pinned along the leg, the edges of the fabric on each side of the dart are perfectly lined up. If one side is sitting lower than the other, your finished dart will jut out a bit on one side of the dart's seam instead of creating an unbroken line.

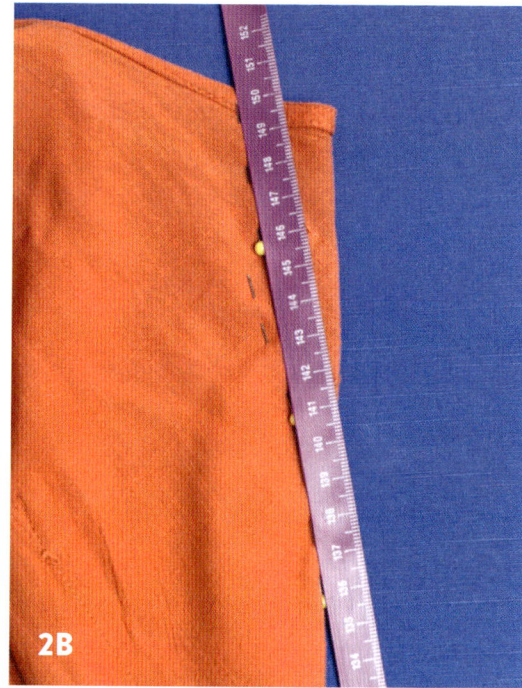

Line up a ruler or straightedge with the top and bottom of your pinned dart leg. Some of your pins are probably skewed along this line, but that's A-OK. Trace along the ruler with chalk or a marker to make your official dart leg and adjust your pins accordingly. Repeat this on any other darts. I recommend placing your pins vertically along the dart legs. This way you can gently try this garment back on and make sure the darts are still lying correctly post-adjustment.

Once you're happy with your dart adjustments, sew these bad boys in place following the instructions in the previous tutorial, Get This Party Darted (page 48).

3A

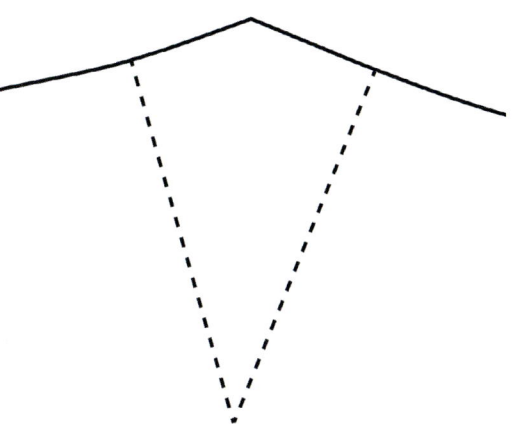

How a dart from a pattern looks before it's sewn.

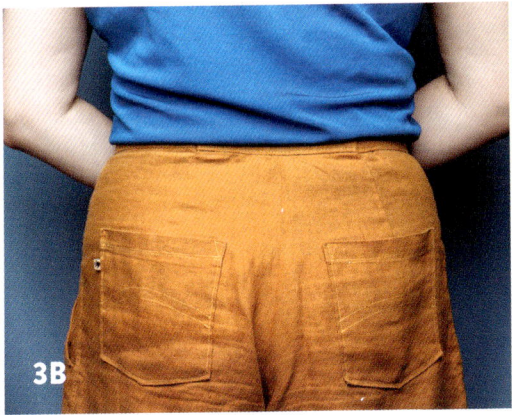

3B

Step 3: Press Your Dart

When it's time to press your darts, review the dart ironing instructions in the previous tutorial on page 51. I always press waistband darts in toward the center and armhole darts upward.

Simple, right? For the most part, but any preexisting garment that you add darts to will come with its own unique challenges.

The Challenges

When you're sewing a dart from scratch on a pattern, the top of the dart is shaped a bit differently than when you add it to a finished garment. On a pattern, the distance between the tops of the two dart legs isn't a straight line. Instead, the fabric curves upward from each dart leg and these curved lines meet in a point above the center of the dart.

The fabric curves in this way so that once the dart is folded to one side, the top edge curves along the same line as the rest of your fabric.

Obviously, it isn't possible to replicate this when you're adding a dart along an existing garment line. I promise we'll all be OK though. This perfect alignment of your dart with the edge of your fabric is most important when this edge is going to be hemmed or attached to another piece of fabric. But seeing as we're not doing either of these things, this is a moot point!

A waistband dart that extends down behind an external pocket, ending before it reaches the bottom of the pocket.

ADDING DARTS TO A WAISTBAND

The biggest problem you'll run into when adding darts to a waistband on pants, shorts, or skirts is the back pockets. I know, who knew pockets could ever be the problem?

Unfortunately, if your garment has welted back pockets (the kind you usually find on the back of dress pants where the opening is marked by a narrow rectangle that sits flush with the rest of the garment), it can be difficult to add darts along your waistband. Your dart has to end before it hits the welt, but that dart will probably be too shallow to lay properly if you do this. The only real work-around to this is to fold the welted pocket opening into your dart and turn this into a—*shudder*—fake pocket. If you must succumb to this fate, I recommend heading to The Outsider: External Pockets (page 167) to replace what you've just lost.

If your garment just has external pockets on the back, that's fine! You just need to be careful to pull the pocket away from your dart as you pin and sew it. You're fine to extend your dart behind your pocket—just make sure the dart ends before the bottom of the pocket. This shouldn't be a problem, as I've never seen a dart extend further than the bottom of a back pocket.

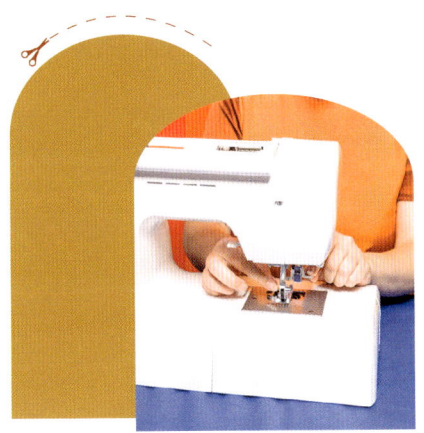

Under an Hour

When I started writing this book, I was focused on big, transformative projects. I've been sewing since I was a kid and have been sharing tutorials online for years. All the while, I've been one of those overachieving perfectionists. I always assume people want something bigger and better from me and forget that a lot of you out there just need someone to gently guide you through the basics. Sometimes you want to turn a sleeping bag into a puffer jacket. Sometimes you just need your favorite T-shirt to be one size smaller.

Our bodies and styles are always changing, which means the way our wardrobe fits us is too. We all have a pair of shorts we've owned since high school that has gotten just a bit too tight. Or a dress that fit perfectly when we bought it, but between washing, wearing, and stretching, it's now running big. Or a T-shirt that we've been rocking as a sleep shirt but have recently decided it's time to rock in the outside world.

These just-a-bit-off garments are the perfect quick and easy introductory projects for honing your new sewing skills. I'm notorious for saying, "Oh, this will only take 30 minutes," right before spending 3 days on a project. However, I'm confident that you can achieve these simple clothing-fit upgrades in under an hour, even as a brand new sewist.

Let It All Out

Sometimes letting go can be tough. But letting your clothes out—that's easy. All you need is a seam ripper, a straight stitch, and a garment with a bit of seam allowance.

I quickly discovered as a 14-year-old that clothes in the teen section were not designed for someone with DD cups. Every time I found something that was perfect everywhere except the chest, I distinctly remember my mom saying, "Let me see how much seam allowance there is." If there was enough, we could buy the top, and my mom would let out the seams. Now the sacred seam ripper has passed to my hands, and I'm the one stalking the aisles of thrift stores whispering to myself, "Let's see how much seam allowance there is."

LEVEL
Beginner

SUGGESTED FABRIC
Any garment with at least one vertical seam. The seam needs to have allowance between the straight stitch and zigzag or overlocking stitch—seams finished exclusively with overlocking can't be made bigger, I'm afraid!

MATERIALS
Too-tight garment with seam allowance
Seam ripper
Ruler or measuring tape
Thread
Sewing machine

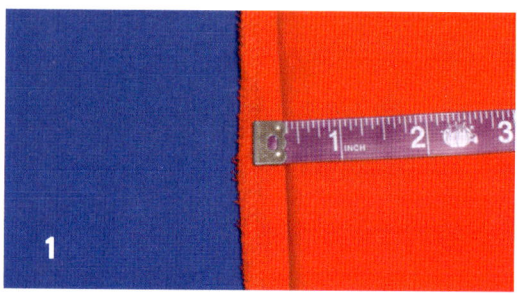

Step 1: Check the Seam Allowance

First let's see how much seam allowance we're working with. The seam allowance is the distance between the straight stitch that attaches two pieces of fabric and the edge of the fabric. Nearly every garment has seams, but the seam allowance can differ drastically. The bigger the seam allowance, the more you can increase the size of your garment.

As you'll remember from Finishing Seams on page 32 (or as you're about to remember when you scurry back and read it before I notice you didn't), seam allowance edges are finished with a zigzag or overlocking stitch. For this project, we're going to keep the overlocking stitches intact, so we're really checking how much space there is between the straight seam stitches and the bottom edge of the overlocking threads. This distance needs to be about ¼ inch (6.5 mm) minimum for this tutorial to be effective in increasing your garment's size.

For most garments, you'll probably let out the side seams, but you don't need to restrict yourself to side seams alone! Garments that are more structured will typically have additional seams like front, back, or princess seams, which shape a garment along your chest and waist. The more seams your garment has, the more you can increase the size. The most important thing to remember when selecting a seam to let out is to also rip the identical seam on the other half of your garment.

Generally speaking, the more expensive the garment, the more seam allowance you have. Those among us that don't need to check price tags on clothes (unrelatable, as I scrutinize a nine-dollar thrift store tag) are more likely to be able to afford getting their clothes tailored. The designer thus gives you extra fabric on the seam so you can get it altered to fit you perfectly.

Conversely, cheaper garments often have smaller seam allowances. Smaller seam allowances mean less fabric used for the garment, which means lower costs to produce.

In many T-shirts or other stretchy knit garments, there is virtually no seam allowance. Instead, the seam is sewn solely with an overlocker, no straight stitch in sight. Alas, there's no expanding these garments without adding more fabric (or putting your arms inside and trying to push through the shirt to stretch it as much as possible).

Oh hey!

If you do in fact need to add fabric to the sides of your shirt, I recommend reading Grow a Pair of Pants (page 129). The tutorial focuses on pants, but I have faith that big brain of yours will be able to adapt the same principles to increasing garments of any kind!

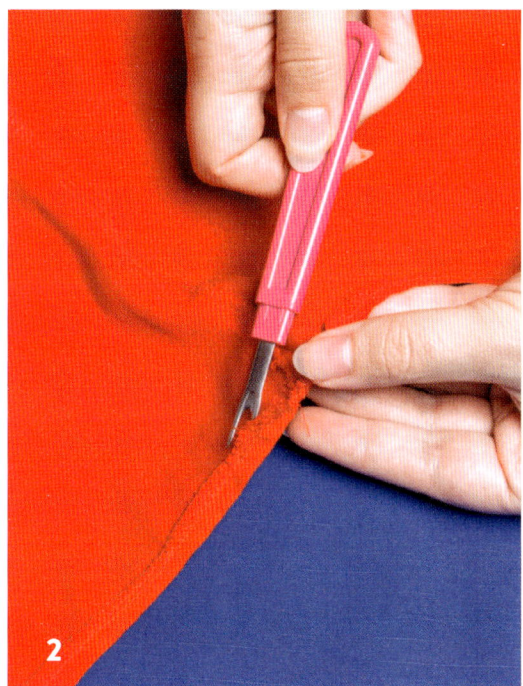 

Step 2: Seam Rip Part of the Hem

This step is the only somewhat annoying part of this project. To access and open your entire seam, you will need to partially open any hems that are folded over these seams. But don't worry, we're only opening a small incision before we sew it back up. And after this you can contact your local hospital and see if they have any surgeon positions open—you're now qualified.

Seam rip your hem about 1 inch (2.5 cm) on each side of the seam you're letting out. You just need to open the hem enough that you can access the seam with your seam ripper in Step 3 and sewing machine in Step 4.

Step 3: Seam Rip the Existing Seam

Now let's get ripping! Grab your seam ripper and remove the straight stitch on each seam you're letting out. Make sure to leave the zigzagged/overlocked finishing stitch fully intact—we still need its support!

If your garment has sleeves and you'd like to let those out as well, just continue seam ripping from the torso up through the sleeve. The torso side seam and the sleeve's underarm seam are typically sewn as one long seam. This means you shouldn't encounter any roadblocks in your seam ripping journey when moving from the torso to the sleeve.

Once you've seam ripped both side seams (or another set of matching seams), you'll have likely gained between ¾ to 1 inch (1.9 to 2.5 cm) of extra breathing room around your garment.

Step 4: Sew the Seam Allowance Narrower

Now we just need to build back up the seam we just tore down. That sounds like we're gaslighting this seam, but really we're just going to replace the straight stitch we ripped with another one closer to the finished edge. We're going to sew about ⅛ inch (3 mm) away from the overlocking stitch. You are more than welcome to measure and mark this, but I wouldn't waste your time. All you need to do is place your needle a hair to the side of the overlocking stitch and maintain that same distance the whole time you resew the seam. I have total faith that even as a new sewist, you will be able to eyeball this. Using a short-medium straight stitch, sew from one end of the ripped seam to the other, making sure to backstitch at the beginning and end.

Step 5: Resew the Hem and Iron

To finish off this short project, we just need to put the hem right back where we found it. Follow the creases that are already in your unrolled hem and fold it back up. Make sure your seam allowance is all laying on one side of the seam as you fold.

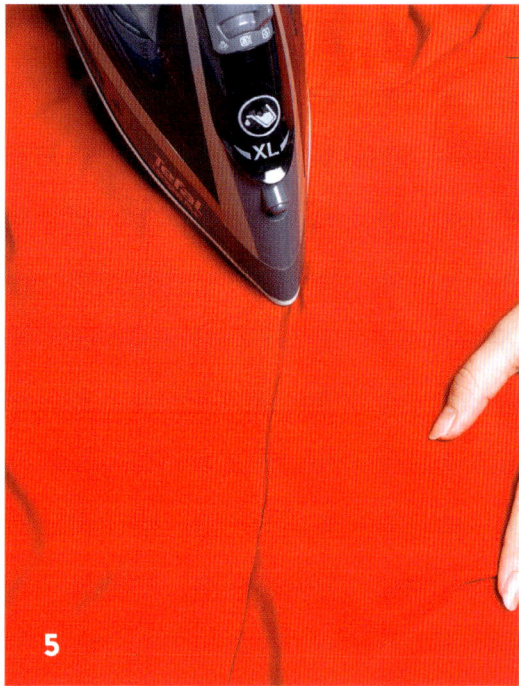

Now with the raw edges tucked back in and ready for bed, use a medium-long straight stitch to sew the hem back together where you seam ripped it. When you're backstitching at the beginning and end, make sure you backstitch over the last three stitches of the thread still holding the rest of your hem together. This will help prevent any more of the hem from coming undone like a toddler who's skipped nap time.

Finally, it's time to give everything a good ol' fashioned press. Iron your new seam and hem flat. The fold of the original seam can be a bit stubborn to press flat, like that one bit of hair you accidentally crimped that now just refuses to straighten. I like to lightly tug the fabric on each side of the seam outward as I iron it to encourage the new seam to lay flat.

Now you can put your garment back on and exhale at last because you no longer have to suck anything in to fit in it. Go forth and be comfortable.

Take It All In

Sometimes the garment you love is only available one size larger than you need. Maybe oversized clothes were all the rage, but you've decided you prefer a more tailored wardrobe. Or maybe you're going to a Spice Girls–themed party and you don't have a single top tiny enough to be any of them (a real situation I recently found myself in). Luckily, reducing the size of a garment is simple. If you can follow a line, you can take in a garment.

LEVEL
Beginner

SUGGESTED FABRIC
Any garment! It's best if the garment has at least one vertical seam that you can follow with your stitching. If you're feeling a bit rebellious, there's no reason you can't follow these same steps with a seamless garment! Avoid ribbed fabric—the ribs can often lie really weirdly if you sew two pieces together at a curve or angle.

MATERIALS
Too-big garment
Similar garment you like the fit of
Chalk or washable marker
Ruler
Pins
Scissors
Thread
Sewing machine
Iron

Step 1: Pin the Garment Smaller

The simplest way to determine how much smaller this garment needs to be is to grab a similar garment with a fit you already love. This just-right garment is going to serve as our pattern. Turn your too-big garment inside out and keep your just-right garment right side out. Make sure any flies, zippers, buttons, etc. are closed on both. Lay your just-right garment on top of your too-big garment.

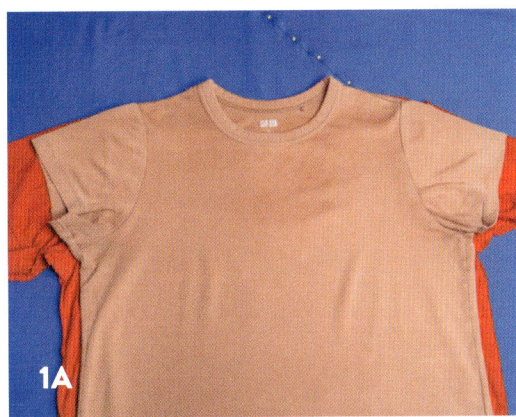

Match up and pin together parts of each garment to serve as anchor points. If you're trying to shrink a shirt or dress, line up the shoulder seams, matching up the top edge of the right-side-out top with the seam of the inside-out top. If you're trying to shrink shorts, pants, or a skirt, match up the top edges of the waistbands. For all garments, ensure the just-right garment is horizontally smack in the center of the too-big garment.

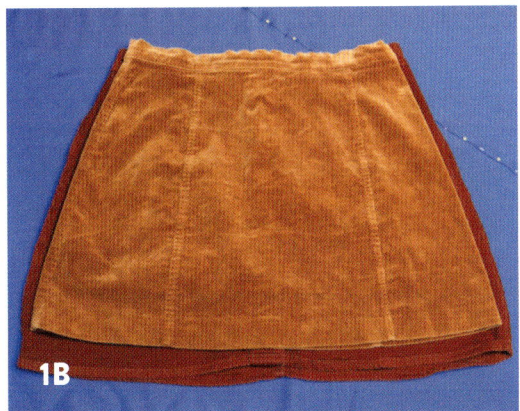

Now grab your chalk or washable marker and draw on your too-big garment, tracing the outer edge of your just-right garment. If your just-right garment is shorter than your too-big garment, that's fine! Line up a ruler with the last several inches of the lines you've drawn, and just continue drawing the line in that same direction until you reach the end of your garment.

Once you've finished tracing, you can throw that just-right garment to the side—there's about to be a new just-right garment in town. Pin both sides of your fabric together along the lines you've drawn on your too-big garment. If you'd like to try on this garment and be absolutely sure it fits the way you like before you sew, place your pins vertically along the lines you've drawn. Then ever so gently try on the garment and check out your new fit in the mirror.

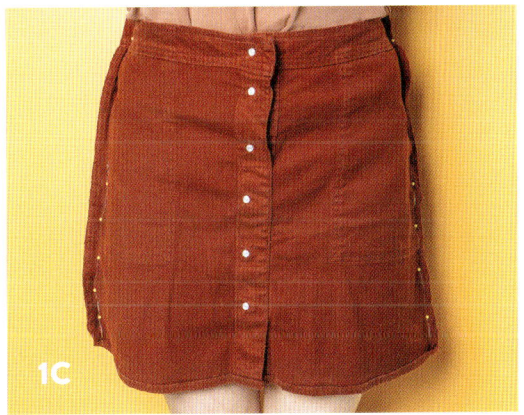

Step 2: Seam Rip Parts of Your Hem

Chances are high that the end of the seam you're about to alter is enclosed in a hem. If you want your altered seam to also be enclosed in a hem, you need to seam rip open parts of the current hem. It's like cleaning your room—it has to get even messier before it gets clean.

Seam rip your hem, beginning 1 inch (2.5 cm) to the left of your traced seam and ending 1 inch (2.5 cm) to the right. You just need to open the hem enough that you can sew along your new side seam. Repeat this on any hems that will be impacted (for instance, the sleeves and bottom of a shirt or dress).

In defense of lazy sewing: Sometimes I think the final product looks better without this step. I absolutely recommend following this step if you will be taking in each seam by a considerable amount—around 1½ inches (3.8 cm) or more. That amount of seam allowance will create visible bulk in your clothing, so you will definitely want to trim, finish, and hide that seam in a hem in the next step.

If, however, you are taking this garment in by less than 1½ inches (3.8 cm), you can take it or leave it with this step. If you're working with a small seam allowance and a knit or delicate fabric, ripping and redoing the hem could leave you with a visible hole or two, so you're better off leaving the hem intact and proceeding to Step 3.

A seam that has been trimmed, refinished, and enclosed inside a hem.

A seam that has been sewn smaller without taking out the original hem or trimming and refinishing the seam.

3A

Oh hey!

What if your too-big garment is only too big in some places but perfect in others? No worries! Begin sewing ½ inch (1.3 cm) above where you will start taking your seam in. We want to stitch exactly along the existing seam, backstitching at the beginning. Sew a few stitches down your existing seam, then gently start to pull your fabric to one side, allowing the needle to slowly drift away from the original seam line and start angling toward the new seam line. Think of this like carefully pulling a blanket away from a sleeping partner or pet rather than yanking a tablecloth away to leave all the dishes magically in place.

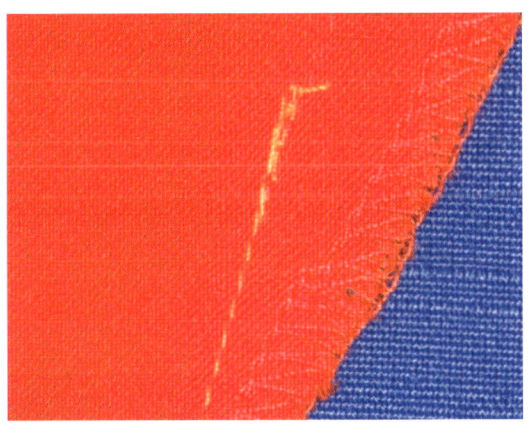

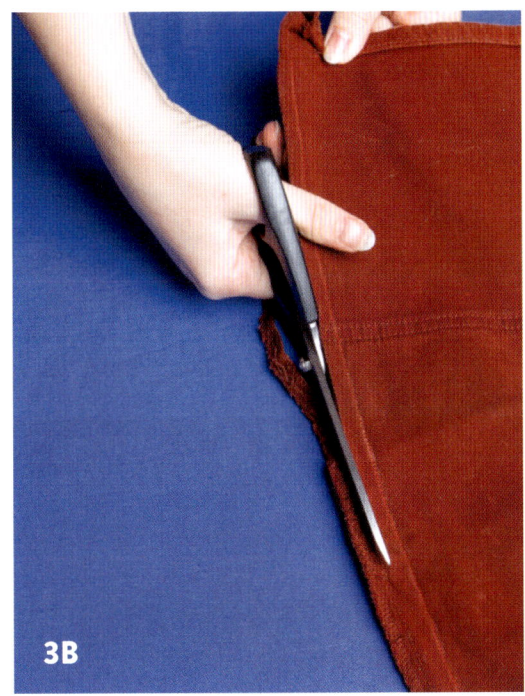

3B

Step 3: Sew and Finish Your New Seam

It's time to sew! Select a short–medium straight stitch on your machine and stitch the two sides of your fabric together along the new seam line that you've drawn. Make sure to backstitch at the beginning and end.

If your new seam is more than ¼ to ½ inch (6.5 mm to 1.3 cm) from your old seam, you'll want to trim the seam allowance and refinish the edges. And even if your new seam isn't far from the old, you're still free to do this! Trim your new seam allowances between ⅜ to ⅝ inch (1 to 1.6 cm) wide, then finish the edges with a zigzag or overlocking stitch (see Finishing Seams, page 32).

Step 4: Finish Your Hems and Iron Your Seams

If you needed to rip any hems open to create your new seams, now is the time to close them back up. Fold them back up following the existing folds, then iron, pin, and sew them in place using a medium–long stitch length and backstitching at the beginning and end. Begin and end your restitching about ¼ inch (6.5 mm) along the original hem's topstitching to ensure you've secured the ends of the stitches we loosened by seam ripping.

Now give your seams and hems a good press with your iron, and you're done! In under an hour, you've transformed a baggy garment into one that fits you like a dream!

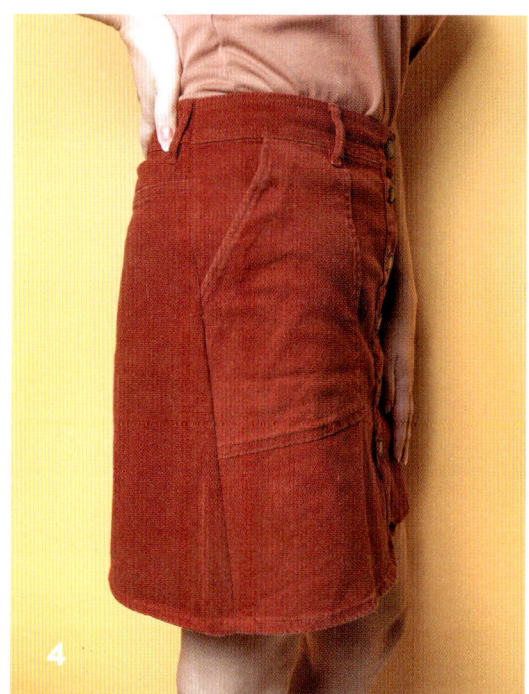

Let's Crop About It: Cropping T-Shirts

Will the crop top ever go out of style? I hope not. And I hope that I still hope this decades from now. They pair great with high-waisted jeans, they're ideal for an '80s aerobics Halloween costume, and they're the best way to disguise stains on the bottom of your T-shirt.

Cropping a T-shirt or sweatshirt seems so simple: cut a straight line across the bottom and voilà! Right? Wrong. Most people who have cropped a shirt know how similar it is to the first time you cut your own bangs: "Hm, still too long, I'll just cut a bit more. Nah, still too long, I'll do a bigger cut this time." And suddenly your bangs are at the top of your forehead and your crop top is nothing but a collar and sleeves. I can't help you with your bangs, but I can save you and your shirts from the overcrop.

LEVEL
Beginner

SUGGESTED FABRIC
Any top you'd prefer to show off more midriff in. Knits are best if you don't want to hem your cropped shirt. See? I'm not totally against working with knits as a beginner! (Only because we're not sewing this.)

MATERIALS
Shirt, sweatshirt, or dress
Belt
Chalk or washable marker
Ruler or measuring tape
Pins
Scissors

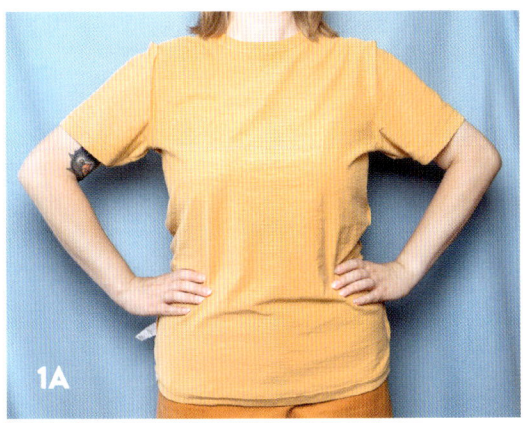

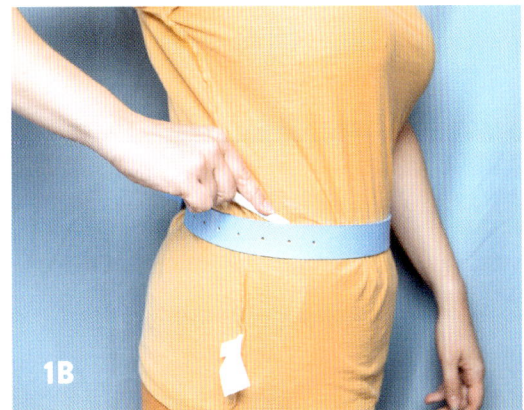

Step 1: Belt and Trace around Your Garment

Turn the garment you're cropping inside out and put it on. Pair it with something on your bottom half that is the typical rise of the bottoms you'll wear with this top. If your typical rise is not high-waisted, I will be supportive but confused—like a mom dropping their teenager off at a screamo concert.

As if we're back in the early 2000s, we're going to put a belt on over our top. Line up the top of your belt with where you'd like your top cropped. Now grab your chalk or marker and trace along the top of your belt, drawing on your garment. You'll see in Step 2 that technically you only need to do this on one-half of your body—from belly button to center back—but I always just go all the way around.

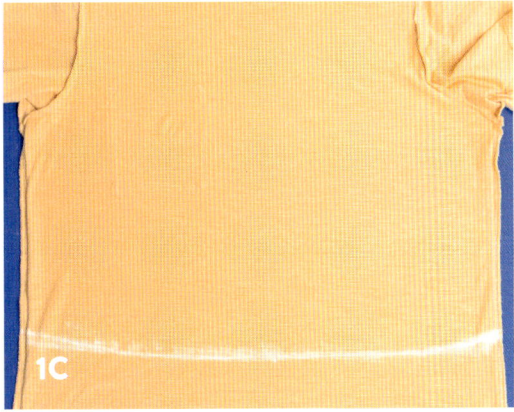

WARNING: If you're a bit chaotic like me and sometimes use nonwashable markers or pens to draw on your fabric, this is *not* the time. We're going to cut below this line, so even though it's on the inside of the garment, make sure you're using something that can easily wipe off or wash out.

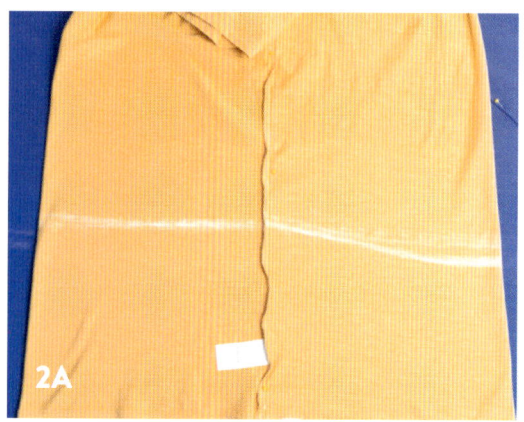
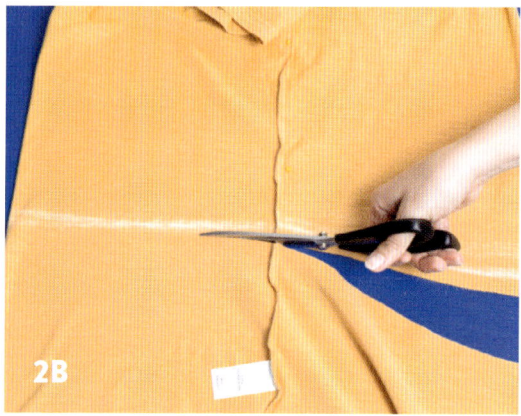

Step 2: Cut the Traced Line

Remove the belt because, unlike in the late 2000s, we're not going to wear this out in public with a fedora and call it fashion. Also take off the garment while you're at it and lay it down on a flat surface. If you have boobs of any kind, it's likely the line you drew on the front of your garment is not straight like you expected, but creates a downward curve in the center. This is exactly what we want. Your shirt needs to be longer in the front than the back to create the appearance of a straight hem. It takes more fabric to go out and over your chest than it does to fall straight down your back, so keeping your shirt longer in the front creates the illusion of a straight line.

Now to crop this bad boy. To create symmetrical cuts, we're going to fold the shirt in half, but probably not in the way you're thinking.

Pinch the center front of your shirt's collar and hem, one in each hand, and pick up your shirt so everything falls below where you're pinching. Now lay your shirt flat. The fabric that covers the right half of your torso (front and back) should be laying on top of the fabric that covers the left half of your torso. The right and left side seams will be in the center of all of this, laying on top of each other. If your shirt doesn't have side seams, match up the armpits. Pin the shirt together a few times along the side seams or armpits to keep your fold in place.

As I mentioned, the line you traced will likely be curved at the center front of the shirt, but it will straighten out toward the side and back. By the time the line reaches the side seam, it will likely be parallel to the bottom hem if not slightly angled up.

Now let's cut 1 inch (2.5 cm) below the line that you traced. I guess you could say this tutorial is a bit . . . ahem . . . below the belt (*ba dum tss*).

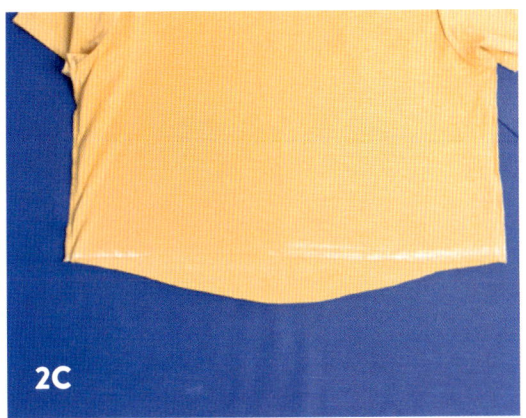
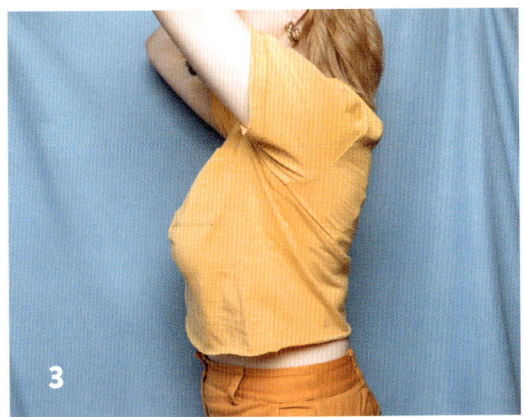

A view from the back—the line along the back is straight while the front is curved.

Even if you think you drew the crop exactly where you want it, heed my warning and give yourself an extra inch. If you're hemming this top, you'll need the extra inch for hemming allowance. If you're not hemming it, you need to account for when you throw this top in the wash and the bottom inevitably rolls up.

You can, of course, use a ruler and measure exactly 1 inch (2.5 cm) below the line you drew (see Let's Get One Thing Straight, page 40), but I always eyeball it. Who really wants a *perfect* cropped shirt, anyway? You can choose your own level of comfort/danger. Following this real or imagined lower line with your scissors, cut through both layers of your garment until you've completely chopped off the bottom.

Step 3: Admire Your Handiwork or Make Adjustments

If you'd like a finished hem, go ahead and do that now (see Hemming & Hawing, page 44). If you're going for the classic crop top and leaving the hem raw, turn your newly cropped top right side out and try it on! If it's blatantly too long for your liking, repeat Steps 1 through 3 to crop it further. If the top is just a little bit too long, I *strongly* encourage you to wash and dry it once to let it reveal its true final length to you before you hack away at it further.

Now match your new crop top with a leotard and leg warmers, and you're ready to throw on some Jane Fonda workouts.

Let's Get Waisted

I highly doubt I'm alone in having a complicated relationship with my waist. Growing up, the words "Show off that tiny waist!" rang through every episode of *What Not to Wear*, every movie makeover montage of the frumpy girl, and every bra-fitting appointment I endured as an uncomfortable 17-year-old. With so much focus on showing off the smallest part of my body, it's no wonder I became obsessed with always wearing belts around my waist. While I've tried to repress the memory, I am *confident* that on multiple occasions I paired a skinny belt with a T-shirt and athletic shorts.

Luckily, the world has shifted away from all tiny waists all the time. And while you don't need to put all your focus on looking your smallest at all times, there are definitely garments a lot of us would prefer to fit our waists better.

I personally never had to struggle with pants being too loose around my waist—honestly, the opposite has always been true. But I have worn many a tent dress in my day. If, like me, some part of your body has prevented you from buying clothes that fit your waist the way they're designed to, this chapter is your opportunity to take the power of fit into your own hands.

In this chapter, I'll teach you how to add waist definition to your clothes without needing to always have a belt within arm's reach. We'll take advantage of elastic and ties for everything, meaning you'll have the option to make things as tight or loose as you please. So, grab your elastic and let's get waisted.

Bring It In: Elasticating Waistbands

If you always find yourself in the center of the dance circle during the opening verse of "Baby Got Back," chances are pants fit either your waist or your hips, but never both. I have a wider-than-average waist (thanks for pointing it out, every size chart ever), so I can't say I relate to this problem. But even when I can't relate, I can commiserate, and probably more importantly, I can teach you how to fix the problem. We're going to add elastic to the back of your waistband to cinch in your clothes while still keeping them stretchy and comfortable.

LEVEL
Confident Beginner

SUGGESTED FABRIC
Shorts, pants, or a skirt with a stiff waistband (preferably with belt loops) that does *not* have a center seam at the back. You'll also need elastic roughly ¼ inch (6.5 mm) narrower than your waistband.

MATERIALS
Shorts, pants, or skirt with a loose waistband

Chalk or washable marker

Scissors

Seam ripper

Elastic

Ruler or measuring tape

Matches, lighter, or candle

Safety pin

Pins

Thread

Sewing machine

Step 1: Cut Open Your Inner Waistband

Identify the belt loops on either side of that darned center-back belt loop you always miss when putting on your belt. On the inside of your waistband, use chalk or a marker to mark a vertical line where these two belt loops are. These will become the entry and exit points for our elastic, so make sure the lines are the height of the elastic, if not a hair taller.

Now to play surgeon and make two precision cuts on the *inside of your waistband only*. Pinch the inside of your waistband and pull it away from the outside of your waistband so we don't accidentally cut it. Snip the inner waistband right at the top of the line you drew, insert your scissors into this entry point, and cut along the entire line. Once you've sliced open both lines, you will have created a channel to guide your elastic through.

Step 2: Seam Rip Your Back Belt Loops

Directing your attention to the outside of the waistband, seam rip just the bottoms of the belt loops that are directly to the left and right of center. Your belt loops should now be dangling, only attached on the top. We're going to reattach these at the end of the project, so don't make more work for yourself by ripping off the top as well.

You may have belt loops that have been attached in two points at the bottom, which is fantastic—for everything except when you're trying to detach the bottom of your belt loops. A super-secure belt loop will be inserted and sewn underneath the exterior waistband and then stitched again at a point 3/8 inch (1 cm) or so below the waistband. If this is the case for you, seam rip the place it's stitched below the waistband. Then use scissors to cut the belt loop as close as physically possible to where it's connected to the waistband. When we reattach this later, we won't be stitching it back under the waistband, but that's OK. Look at other pairs of pants you own, and I guarantee you will see loads of belt loops with raw edges.

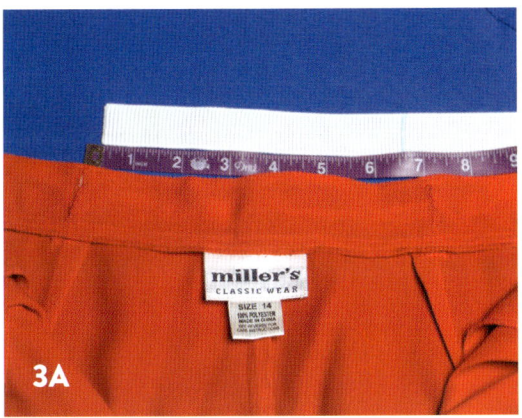

3A

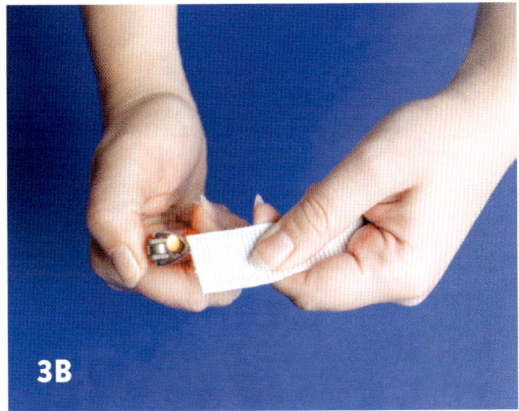

3B

Step 3: Thread Your Elastic through Your Waistband

Grab your elastic. It can be an entire roll for now; we'll only cut the elastic once we've attached one side to our pants. For now, we'll measure and mark the elastic for the maximum amount you'll need. Measure the distance between your two waistband cuts. At most, your elastic will be 75 percent of this distance, but it will probably be even less. Using this formula, multiply the amount in the parentheses first, then add ½ inch (1.3 cm) to account for the "seam allowance" on both ends (there's not actually a seam, it just needs to extend slightly beyond your open cuts).

(Distance between two cuts x 0.75) + ½ inch (1.3 cm)

Starting at the end of your elastic, measure the result of this formula and mark it on your elastic. Now you'll have a solid jumping-off point when you decide your official elastic length later.

For all you pyromaniacs out there, I have incredible news. It's time to grab a match, lighter, or candle. We're melting elastic. Elastic is made of plastic threads that very easily come unraveled (relatable). To prevent the unraveling

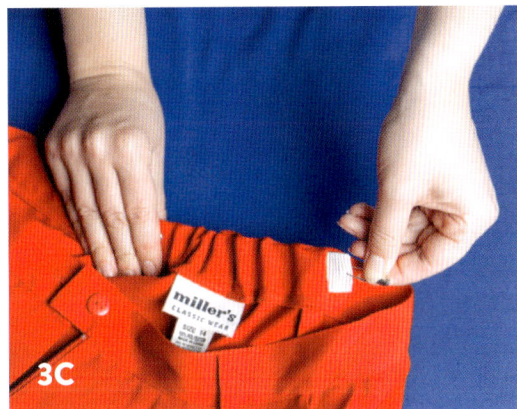

3C

(I take medication for mine), slowly guide the end of your elastic back and forth once in front of an open flame. This will melt the ends of the elastic shut—just make sure you don't hold it too close to the flame, because it can catch fire. And if that happens, you're banned from singing "We Didn't Start the Fire" for a whole month. Those are just the rules.

Attach a safety pin to the end of your elastic. This pin is going to serve as the elastic's headlamp as we take it on a caving expedition through the waistband channel. Put the elastic in one of the open cuts and thread it through your waistband channel until you can pull it out of the open cut on the other side. Once it's all the way through, you can take off the safety pin and, if you're like me, put it down and promptly lose it forever.

LET'S GET WAISTED

If you pull out bits of thin fabric from your waistband with your elastic and safety pin, don't panic. This is interfacing that was attached to your waistband to make it sturdier. But have no fear—your waistband is going to be even sturdier now that there's elastic in there. It's that whole "one door closes and another opens" thing.

Step 4: Sew One End of the Elastic in Place

Until further notice, when I refer to the end of the elastic and the open cut, I am talking exclusively about the side we just pulled the safety-pinned end of the elastic to. Just leave the other end of the elastic be—its time will come.

The end of your elastic should be ¼ inch (6.5 mm) beyond the open cut, but still inside the waistband. Pin the elastic in place along the open cut and sew it in place. When sewing this at your machine, make sure to pull the detached belt loop out and away from where you're stitching. Using a straight stitch and a short stitch length, sew from the top to the bottom of the elastic along the center of the open cut. Your stitch should be going through the elastic and the outside of the waistband.

Now to close the opening you cut. Lay the edges of your cut flat so that they're kissing. Then yell, "Get a room!" On your sewing machine, select the zigzag stitch and a maximum stitch length of 1. If your zigzag stitches come in multiple widths, choose the wider option. We're going to use this stitch to close the open side of the cut and completely cover the raw edges we've created. Once again, we're stitching through both layers of the waistband, making sure the detached belt loop is safely removed from the line of fire (stitching). Starting from one end of the cut, sew along the entire opening, starting and stopping around ⅛ inch (3 mm) beyond the ends and backstitching at the beginning and end. As you sew, the zig should be on one side of the cut and the zag on the other. Or in layman's terms, the needle should alternate sewing on the left and right sides of the opening.

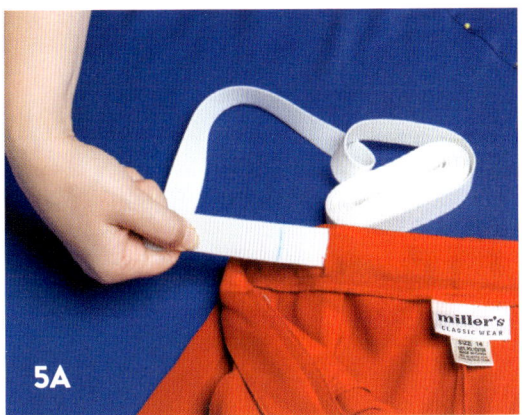

Step 5: Attach the Other Side of the Elastic

It is officially further notice. I'm now referring to the other end of the elastic and open cut.

Time to switch our attention to the unattached end of the elastic. This portion of the project is a bit of an exercise in guessing and testing. Pull the elastic tight until the mark we made in Step 3 matches up with the center of the open cut and pin it in place. But don't you dare cut that excess elastic off yet.

If you're working with a long roll of elastic, hold the excess in your hand while trying on your garment, and see if the waistband is tight enough (or too tight). If the fit isn't perfect yet, take the garment off and either tighten or loosen the elastic further. Then try the garment back on until your inner Goldilocks finds the fit just right. I personally always find it best to pull the elastic a little bit tighter than you think is comfortable because chances are it will stretch out once you're wearing your garment.

Once you're pleased with the tightness of the waistband, you can trim off the excess elastic, leaving ¼ inch (6.5 mm) additional elastic to extend beyond the cut. Get your flame back out, melt this end of the elastic (ensuring you've pulled the end far away from your flammable garment), and repeat Step 4 to attach it and close the opening.

Step 6: Reattach the Belt Loops

Now to pull an All-American Rejects and keep this elastic our dirty little secret. We're going to hide our elastic-securing stitches by sewing the bottoms of the belt loops back in place. You should be able to easily see where the belt loops were originally attached because they will have left prominent stitch marks.

The belt loop fabric will probably be too bulky and the surface area too small to pin the belt loops in place. You can get by stitching them without pinning in place, but if you need that security, pin the center of the belt loop down to help you keep the bottom of the loop straight.

Using a medium–long straight stitch, sew across the bottoms of your belt loops two to three times. Because belt loops are a bit bulky, it can be difficult to force them through your home sewing machine. I find it easier to feed them through the machine by manually turning the handwheel instead of using the foot pedal. Alternatively, if you have the patience to switch your presser foot to a walking foot (see Presser Feet, page 29), you'll have a much easier time feeding this through.

You're now left with a waistband that's as snatched as you but still stretches when you sit down, eat bread, drink anything with bubbles, or generally exist.

Around the Bend: Elasticating Tops

If you want waist definition but also want to be able to go out for pizza and beer and not be suffocated by your top or dress while you're sitting down, elastic is your best friend. The best thing about adding elastic to your clothes is that the customization possibilities are endless! You can add a single strip of elastic to the front of your top to make a cute little gather. You can add elastic just to the sides to cinch everything in. Or you can add several strips of elastic around the entire circumference of your top for a cute smocked effect.

In this tutorial, we're going to make a fully cinched waist using encased elastic. We're focusing on the waist in this tutorial, but you can take these skills and add encased elastic to sleeves and pant cuffs as well.

LEVEL

Intermediate

SUGGESTED FABRIC

You'll need a piece of elastic about ¼ to 1½ inches (6.5 mm to 3.8 cm) wide that's long enough to wrap around your waist. We'll thread the elastic through a channel of fabric inside the garment. The fabric won't be seen, so it doesn't need to match your garment's color—meaning this is a great project to use up the fabric you bought impulsively that you don't actually like that much. I suggest using a woven fabric that is incredibly easy to iron. You'll need a lot of length, which you'll learn more about in Step 2.

MATERIALS

Flowy or baggy dress, shirt, or jumpsuit

Elastic

Scissors

Chalk or washable marker

Ruler and measuring tape

Elastic channel fabric

Pins

Iron

Matching thread

Sewing machine

Matches, lighter, or candle

Safety pin

Sticky tape

> **Make it your own:** There's no need to stop at just one elastic band! I love the look of multiple lines of narrow elastic wrapped around the waist, so I added a second line at the end of this project. If you want to replicate this, just repeat all the steps as you go. Just make sure to wait until you've finished sewing absolutely everything else before you thread any elastic through. Otherwise, it will make it very tricky for you to repeat all the steps!

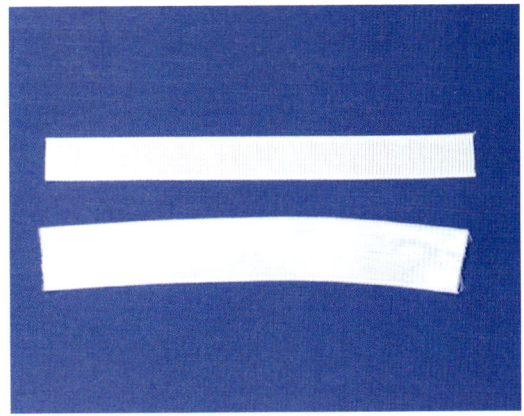

Top: Ribbed elastic. Bottom: Woven elastic.

Step 1: Prepare Your Elastic

Determine the width of your elastic to best fit your body and aesthetic. I recommend keeping the width between ¼ inch to 1½ inches (6.5 mm to 3.8 cm)—any wider and I think it becomes uncomfortable, but you do you. My favorite type of elastic is ribbed elastic because it's resistant to rolling and twisting. A basic braided or woven elastic will also do the trick just fine but is more prone to rolling or folding over, especially when it's wider.

To figure out the length of your elastic, it's best to wrap the elastic around your waist until it fits perfectly comfortably. However, if you don't feel like guessing and testing, a great guideline is that your elastic should be 75 percent of your waist circumference. This will give you a piece of elastic that cinches you without squeezing you. To calculate your elastic length, measure around your waist, multiply by 0.75, and add an inch (2.5 cm) to account for a ½-inch (1.3-cm) seam allowance on each side.

(Waist measure x 0.75) + 1-inch (2.5-cm) total seam allowance

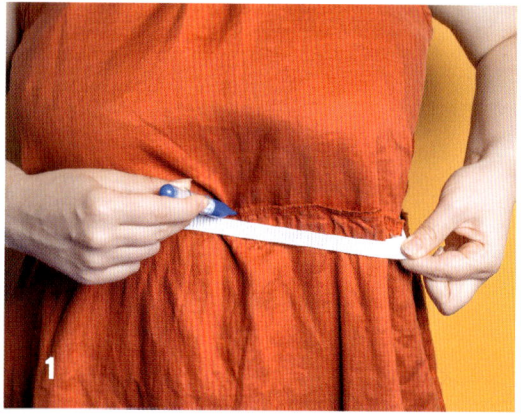
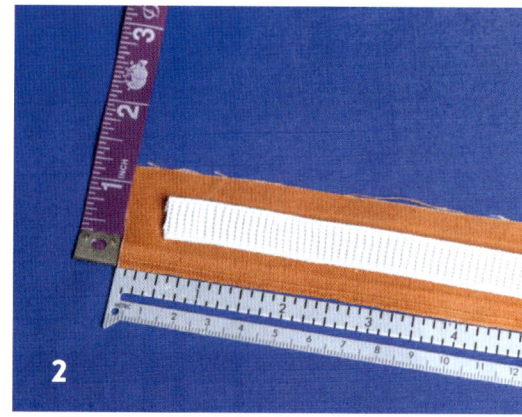

Now to determine the placement of the elastic. Try on your flowy dress, shirt, or jumpsuit inside out. Grab your elastic, wrap it around your waist, look in the mirror, give yourself a wink, and adjust the elastic until it's positioned just to your liking. Using chalk or a marker, mark the garment at the top of the elastic in four spots: center front, center back, and on each side.

Step 2: Prepare the External Fabric for Your Channel

Our elastic is going to be fully encased in a fabric channel, kind of like a sausage but with a wildly different flavor profile. To pave the way for this channel, use a ruler and chalk or a marker to draw a line connecting the four marks you've just drawn. This line should go around the circumference of your garment and will serve as a guide for pinning the fabric channel.

The fabric channel will be sewn to the inside of the garment. To ensure this encasing fabric doesn't have any raw edges that can unravel with wear and tear, we'll be folding under and ironing all of the edges before we sew it onto the garment. If you're keeping score, you've figured out that this is going to require a fair bit of prep work.

To determine how long your encasing fabric needs to be, grab your measuring tape and measure the length of the line you've just drawn around your garment. Add an additional 1 inch (2.5 cm) to this measurement to allot for folding the ends under, and you have the length of your encasing fabric:

Garment circumference + 1 inch (2.5 cm)

The width of your encasing fabric should be about ¼ inch (6.5 mm) wider than your elastic, plus another ½ inch (1.3 cm) wider to account for the fabric we need to fold under and iron. So, your encasing fabric width formula is:

Width of elastic + ¾ inch (1.9 cm)

Now cut out a rectangle of encasing fabric that is the length and width you calculated.

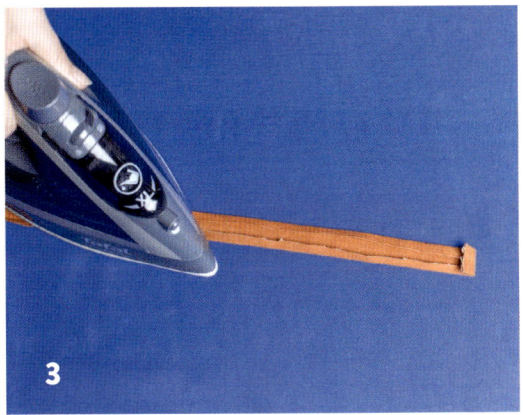

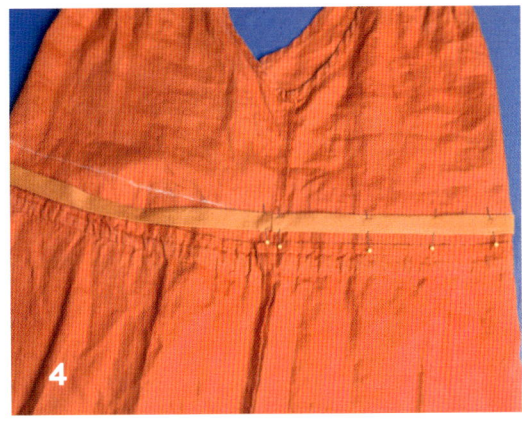

Step 3: Iron the Encasing Fabric

Using a little something I prepared earlier—Let's Get One Thing Straight (page 40)—as a guide, fold and iron your excess fabric. With the right side of your encasing fabric facing down, fold over and iron ¼ inch (6.5 mm) on each of your long sides of fabric. This is a great time to listen to a podcast, practice saying the alphabet backward, or contemplate the meaning of life, because this ironing can take a while.

Once you've completed more ironing than I did in all my teenage years combined, fold over ½ inch (1.3 cm) on each of the short sides of the fabric and iron these down as well.

Step 4: Pin the Encasing Fabric to Your Garment

The prep work is almost over! Right after we do this entire other step of prep work. Sorry, I wanted you to feel joy for a moment. Did it work?

With your garment inside out, take your encasing fabric and lay it down so all the edges are folded underneath. Line up the fabric's top folded edge with the line you drew around the circumference. Line up the short end of your fabric with one of your garment's side seams.

Now wrap the fabric around the garment, line up the other short end so it's flush with the first one, and pin it in place. With a starting and ending point established, we're ready to pin the rest of the encasing fabric. Pin your fabric to your garment every few inches, always lining up the fabric's top fold with the line you drew. Be careful not to accidentally pin through both sides of the garment at once, or getting in and out will become very tricky.

Step 5: Sew the Encasing Fabric to Your Garment

Now this time we're really finished with the prep work and ready to get on with sewing! Select a medium-length straight stitch and thread that matches your garment. This thread will be fully visible on the outside of your garment, so make sure you like the way it looks.

With your garment still inside out, edgestitch along the top and bottom of the encasing fabric, backstitching at the beginning and end. Your stitching should start and end at the side seams where the ends of your encasing fabric are pinned. Do *not* sew these short ends closed. Just like with pinning, make sure you're only sewing the fabric to a single layer of your garment.

Your construction of the fabric tunnel is complete! The openings along the short ends are the entrance and exit to this tunnel, where the only tolls are those on your fingers as you thread the elastic through. Okay, it's not that dramatic, but your fingers may get a bit tired in Step 6.

Step 6: Thread the Elastic through the Fabric Tunnel

Finally, let's add this elastic to our garment. For my favorite prep step in sewing, grab your elastic and some source of flame—a match, lighter, or candle. You'll likely see that your elastic has frayed a bit (or a lot) where it's been cut, and if it hasn't, it will soon. To prevent the fray (not the band), slowly guide the end of your elastic back and forth once in front of an open flame. Elastic is made of plastic, so the flame will melt the ends together. Just be careful not to hold it too close to the flame for too long! Otherwise, your elastic will catch fire and you'll have to answer "What's burning?" questions from anyone you live with.

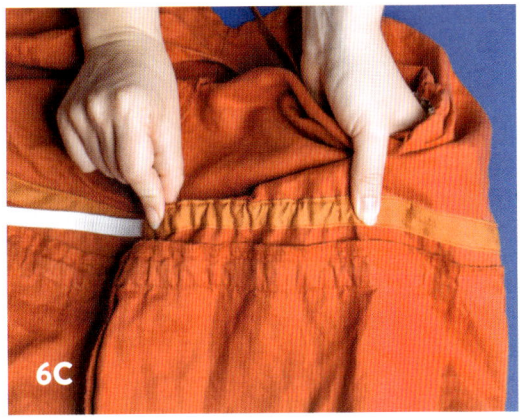

Once your elastic edges are melted shut, attach a safety pin to one end. The safety pin functions as a dull needle to thread your elastic through the fabric tunnel. I highly encourage you to actually get a safety pin for this instead of using what you have lying around the house. There are only so many times a girl can try to rewrap a piece of elastic around a bobby pin while it's trapped in the middle of a fabric tunnel. I also strongly recommend wrapping a piece of tape around the safety pin's closure to prevent it from opening inside the channel.

Threading the elastic through the fabric tunnel can feel like being stuck in a traffic jam. Put on your favorite podcast and go slowly as you push your safety pin forward, push a chunk of fabric onto it, and then pinch the safety pin as you pull the gathered fabric down the elastic.

Once you've pulled the elastic far enough through the tunnel that the other end of elastic has finally reached the opening, make sure to pin it securely to the opening. If you don't, you'll be trying to fish the elastic back out of the tunnel.

Continue pulling the elastic until it comes out the other end of the tunnel. Hooray! You made it through! Pull both ends of elastic a couple inches out of their respective tunnel openings so we can sew the ends together.

Oh hey!

Sometimes all the prep work in the world can't prevent a traffic jam in the fabric tunnel. If your safety pin in some way comes loose and causes a traffic jam of elastic and sharp pin in your fabric tunnel, don't panic. The more you panic, the more you'll stab yourself with the pin and accidentally drop blood on your garment (this has happened to me more than once). You just have to perform some minor surgery.

Grab your seam ripper and remove several of the stitches along the tunnel where the safety pin is stuck. Once you've removed enough stitching, you'll be able to pull the safety pin and the end of the elastic through the opening and reattach or replace the problem safety pin. Then pop it back through the opening and continue guiding it through the tunnel. You'll just need to go back and straight stitch over the bit you ripped open. Luckily, the way the fabric will bunch together once it's elasticated will camouflage the bit you have to resew.

Step 7: Sew the Seams Closed

Take the last ½ inch (1.3 cm) of each end of the elastic, lay them flat on top of each other, and pin them together. By stacking the seam allowance, we avoid creating any extra bulk in the elastic.

Using a medium-length straight stitch, we're going to sew together our seam allowance with a square. Starting in one corner of the elastic that's lying on top, stitch down the edge of the elastic, turn your elastic 90 degrees, sew down the next side, and so on until you're back at the start. When you're back to the beginning, turn the elastic 45 degrees and stitch a diagonal line through the box, backstitching at the end. Now you have a flat, secure seam allowance that isn't going to pull apart when your elastic stretches. Stretch your garment along the elastic to suck any elastic hanging outside of the tunnel back inside.

Clearly, it doesn't have to look pretty; it just needs to hold the elastic together.

7A

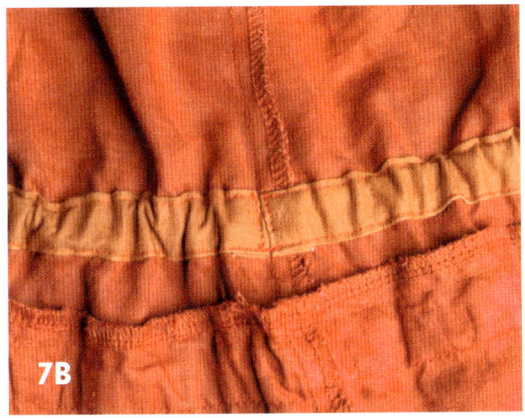

7B

7C

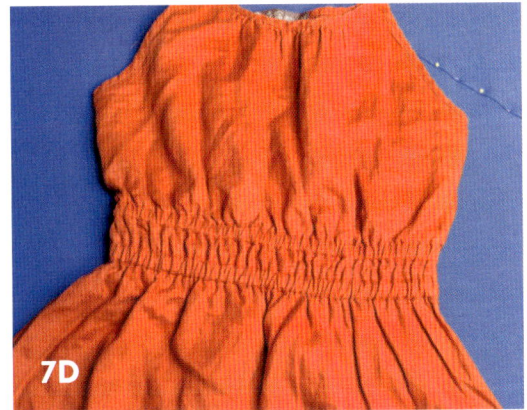

7D

Finally, we can close up the openings to the tunnel. If you want a super-clean finish, you can hand stitch the two open ends together just on the inside of the garment. For those of us that can't be bothered with hand stitching, select a medium-length straight stitch on your machine. Edgestitch each of the short ends closed, backstitching at the beginning and end.

With the tunnel officially closed to all vehicles, your elastic waistband is complete! Now you're ready to repeat this process on sleeves, pants, scrunchies, or whatever else you dream of elasticating.

All Tied Up

I grew up with a huge chest that made every shirt, dress, and jumpsuit look like a tent because the fabric would just take a vertical cliff dive off the tip of my tits. I was desperate to give myself any waist definition, and thus entered my wardrobe staple: the belt. You could not find me wearing a dress in the 2010s without an accompanying skinny belt. Nowadays I can survive without a belt glued to my waist, but I do still love a garment with a tasteful tie.

Adding a tie to your garment can be a game changer. You have the option to tie it as loosely or tightly as you want, completely controlling the amount of waist definition. It also visually trumps a belt, in my humble opinion. Perhaps my biggest qualm with adding an external belt to an outfit is that it can visually cut you in half. With a tie, you can visually create a longer line, either by choosing an identical fabric or by tying the garment just in the back so the front is an unbroken line.

LEVEL

Intermediate

SUGGESTED FABRIC

You'll need *looong* pieces of fabric to create your ties for this one! Depending on your aesthetic, you can choose fabric in an identical or wildly different color to your garment. If you're desperate to work with knit fabrics, this is a good project to try it on. You'll need to do minimal sewing on the flowy/baggy garment itself, and the ties will be wrapped around your body and knotted or tied in a bow, so it won't be as noticeable if you end up with wavy seams.

MATERIALS

Flowy or baggy top, dress, or jumpsuit

Tie fabric

Measuring tape and ruler

Chalk or washable marker

Scissors

Pins

Thread

Sewing machine

Straw and chopstick or loop turner

Iron

Seam ripper

Positive attitude toward math

> **Heads-up:** If you plan to make a skinny tie (similar to a spaghetti strap in width), and you've never loop turned before, read Step 4 first so you know what you're in for. I always encourage you to try something new and challenging, but I want you to have all the facts up front!

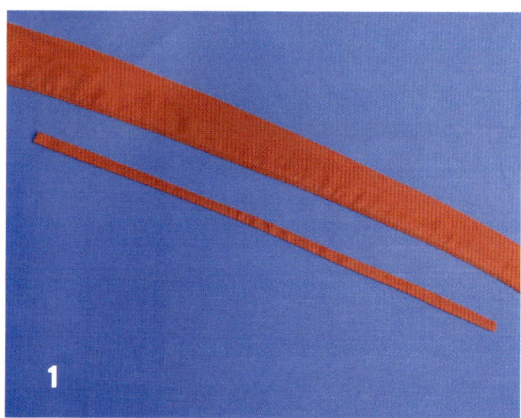

Step 1: Determine the Length and Width of Your Tie

Decide how skinny or thick you'd like your ties to be. A skinny tie is a good option if you want this tie to be primarily functional without drawing much attention (like the way I hoped nobody would ever notice I replaced a broken buckle on my black boots with a bulldog clip I found at work). If you want the tie to be a feature of your outfit, opt for something at least 2 inches (5 cm) thick. There are dresses on the market with solid 6- to 8-inch (15.5- to 20.5-cm) waist ties, so don't be afraid to go big or go home with this!

Next up, let's decide the length of the tie. I'll tell you this up front—this tie needs to be longer than you think. I've made many a tie too short in my life, beginning way back when I first cut ribbon to tie up a present without my mom's help. I don't think the "bow" on that present could fit any dictionary definition of a bow.

Do you intend to tie this tie into a bow or a knot, or both, depending on your mood? Will you tie it solely in the front or back of your garment, or do you want to wrap it around the circumference of your waist before tying it? How far do you want the ends to hang down once it's tied—just a few inches, a whole foot, past the bottom hem of your garment? Is anybody else suddenly singing "Do Your Ears Hang Low?"

The formula to find the length of each of your two ties is:

Distance around the body + length to tie the knot/bow + length below the knot/bow

To find the **distance around the body**:

- Measure the circumference of your waist with a tape measure.
- If you're tying this just in the front or back, divide the circumference by 4.
- If you're tying this across your front and then tying in the back (or vice versa), multiply the circumference by 0.75.
- If you're tying this across your front, then back, then tying in the front (or vice versa), multiply the circumference by 1.25.

To find the **length to tie the knot/bow**:

- If you're tying this in a knot, add 3.5 inches (9 cm).
- If you're tying this in a bow, add 8.5 inches (22 cm). (This will give you a 2.5-inch [6.4-cm] long bow, so if you want a bigger bow, add more length.)

To find the **length below the knot/bow**:

- This is entirely up to you! If you're not sure, I recommend 12 inches (31 cm). Don't forget, you can always shorten this later!

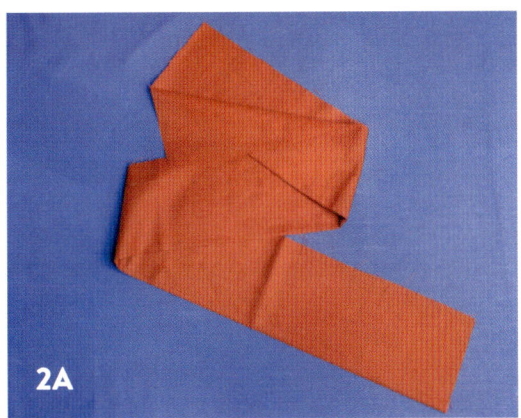

2A

Step 2: Cut Out Your Ties

It's been fun having you along for this book, but it's time to cut ties. (Please keep reading this book and my sewing puns.) Grab your tie fabric and fold it in half so we can cut both ties at the same time. On one side of your fabric, you'll need to draw a rectangle.

**Rectangle length:
Tie length from Step 1 + 1 inch (2.5 cm)**

**Rectangle width:
(Desired tie width x 2) + 1 inch (2.5 cm)**

The extra inch on each side will account for a ½-inch (1.3-cm) seam allowance. Cut your rectangle out of both layers of fabric.

If your tie is 2 to 3 inches (5 to 8 cm) wide, a plain rectangle of fabric will serve you perfectly. If your tie is any wider than 3 inches (8 cm), I'd recommend making it narrower at the end of the tie. To do this, take one of your rectangles, fold it in half lengthwise, and pin it in several spots to prevent it from moving around.

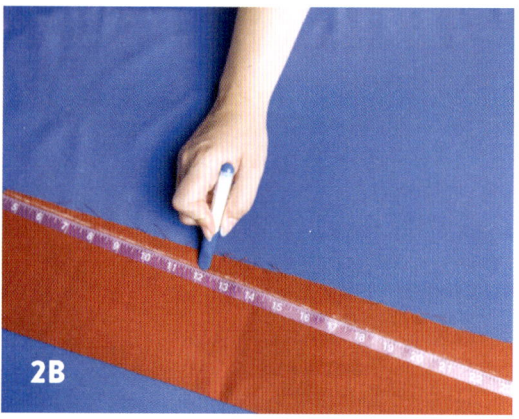

Decide how narrow you'd like your tie to be at the end. I recommend between 50 to 75 percent of the width of the other end of your tie. On one end of the folded rectangle, measure up from the fold and mark how narrow you'd like it to be. Measure ½ inch (1.3 cm) up from this mark and mark again to account for the seam allowance. Using a straightedge, draw a line from this mark to the top corner of the other end of your rectangle. Cut along this line through both layers of your rectangle, then repeat on your second rectangle.

Step 3: Sew Your Rectangles into Ties

Time to sew these rectangles! Fold the rectangle lengthwise with the right sides touching. Line up the raw edges of the rectangle and pin them together. We're going to sew the long edge and the short edge at the end of the tie. We'll keep the edge of the rectangle that attaches to the garment open.

Select a short straight stitch on your sewing machine. You're going to pull these ties a lot when you wear this garment, so we need a small stitch length to keep these seams tight and secure. Start sewing the long edge of the rectangle from the edge that will attach to the garment, leaving a ½-inch (1.3-cm) seam allowance and backstitching at the beginning. Sew a straight line down the long edge until you're ½ inch (1.3 cm) from the rectangle corner. Turn your fabric 90 degrees, then continue sewing all the way down the short edge of the rectangle, again with ½ inch (1.3 cm) seam allowance. Backstitch at the end.

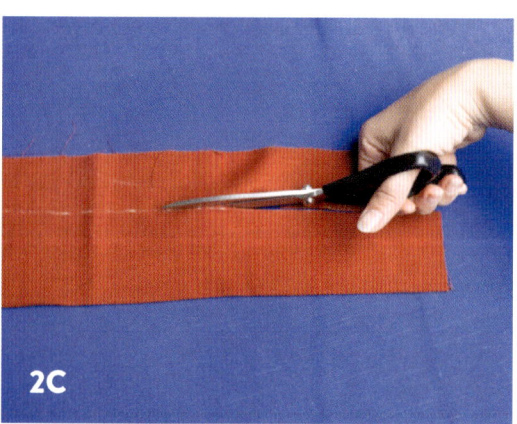

Now we just need to finish these seams. First, clip the two corners on the stitched short edge of your rectangle. To clip the corners, cut off a triangle of seam allowance on the outside of the stitched corner. This will prevent the points of our ties from being bulky when we turn the ties right side out.

Finish the seams on the two sewn edges with a zigzag stitch or overlocker. If you're making a skinny tie, before you finish the seams, you'll need to trim down your seam allowance until it's narrower than your folded rectangle.

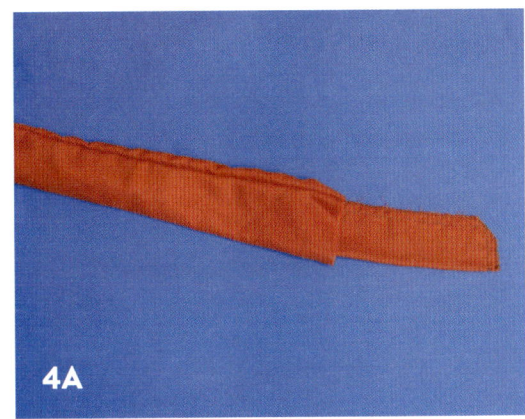

Step 4: Turn the Rectangles Right Side Out

Now for a task that makes me feel the same way seam ripping does: loop turning. Loop turning is when you take an inside-out tube of fabric and turn it right side out. It is also my Achilles' heel. Don't be afraid though—so many sewists are great at loop turning. It's just one of those things I'll never be good at (like knowing when to stop oversharing when I meet a new person).

The wider your rectangle, the easier it will be to loop turn. Which sadly means that the narrower the rectangle, the harder it is to loop turn. Our work starts at the short edge of the rectangle that is stitched closed. We need to push this end down inside the stitched rectangle.

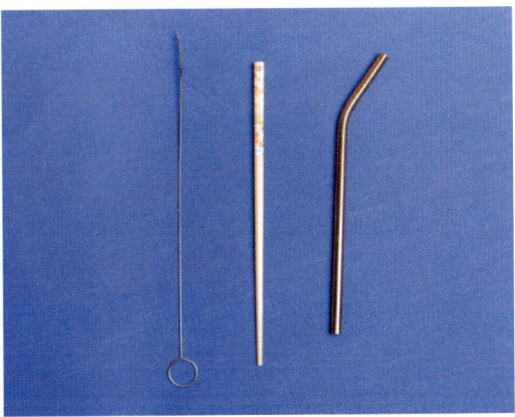

Some suggested tools for this step. Left to right: A loop-turner, chopstick, and straw.

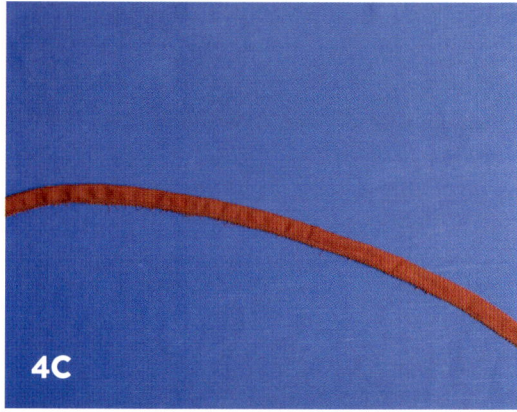

For a wider rectangle, pinch each side of your folded rectangle and pull the sides away from each other. Then find a spare finger to push the edge of the rectangle into the space you've created. From here, grab a long narrow object like a chopstick or a straw. Stick this object into the turned-in end of the rectangle, then stand the object up on a flat surface.

Use your thumb and index finger to slide the inside-out fabric down the object. Keep wiggling this fabric down until the short edge of the rectangle births itself from the other end of the rectangle. At this point, use your object to gently poke out the corners of the rectangle's short end.

From here, you can forgo the object. Hold on to the right-side-out end of the rectangle with one hand while continuing to pull down the inside-out fabric with your other hand. Continue until the whole rectangle is right side out.

For a narrow rectangle, grab a straight straw and a narrow object like a chopstick or skewer that can fit all the way through the straw. Stand the straw up on a flat surface and pull the inside-out rectangle onto the straw. You'll need to scrunch the fabric to get it all to fit on the straw. Or combine multiple straws together like a kid making a wildly impractical megastraw.

Once you've pulled the fabric all the way around the straw with the sewn short edge right at the top, take your chopstick or skewer to push the short edge inside the straw. Continue pushing the fabric into the straw while simultaneously sliding the rest of the inside-out fabric onto the chopstick or skewer. Be gentle with this process to avoid poking a hole through the short edge of your rectangle.

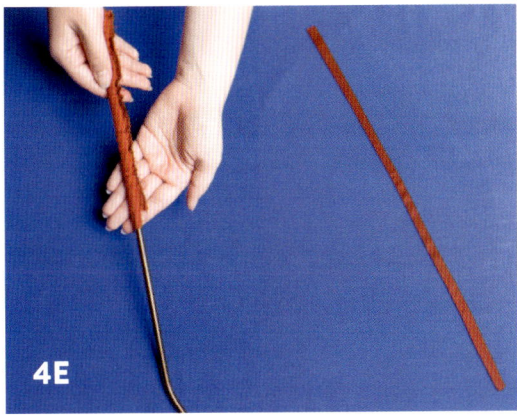

Keep wiggling this fabric down until the short edge of the rectangle appears right side out on the other end of the straw.

At this point, use your object to gently poke out the corners of the rectangle's short end. From here, you can forgo your chopstick or similar object. Pinch the right-side-out end of your rectangle and pull it through your straw, while using your other hand to shimmy any still inside-out fabric up the straw.

Wide and narrow rectangles: Once both your ties are turned right side out, lay them down with the seam on one side, and iron the ties flat.

As an optional final step to prepare the ties, topstitch along your ties ⅛ inch (3 mm) in from the seam.

Step 5: Attach the Ties to Your Garment

Let's tie this project up! Grab some pins and your garment—it's time to play "Guess and Test." Try on your garment right side out and pin your ties to your side seams where you think they'll work best. If you accidentally stick your side with a pin while attaching these, consider this your tetanus shot reminder. With the ties pinned, try all the ways you plan to tie this garment to make sure the ties are exactly where you need them. If they don't work where you first pinned them, pin, pin again until you get your perfect fit.

Once you've found the ideal placement for your ties, take your garment off so we can get seam ripping. Mark on your garment's side seam where the top and bottom of your ties are so you can unpin them from your garment. Now seam rip your garment between the two marks (Let 'Er Rip, page 35).

Put the unstitched end of your tie through the garment's new opening. My preference is to have the seam of the tie facing down so it's less noticeable on the finished garment. There's nothing wrong with the seam being visible though, if that's your vibe! Now turn the garment inside out so we can give all our attention to the seam.

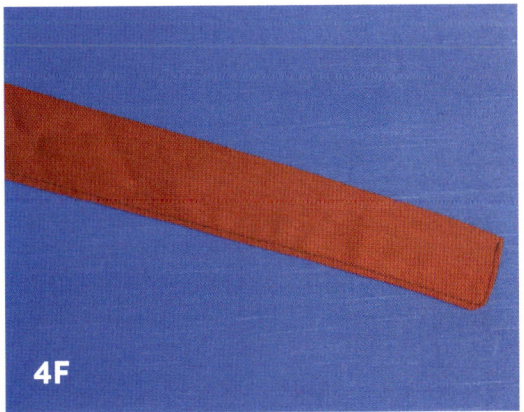

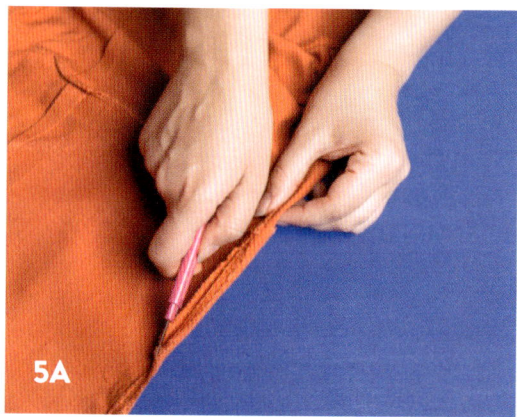

5A

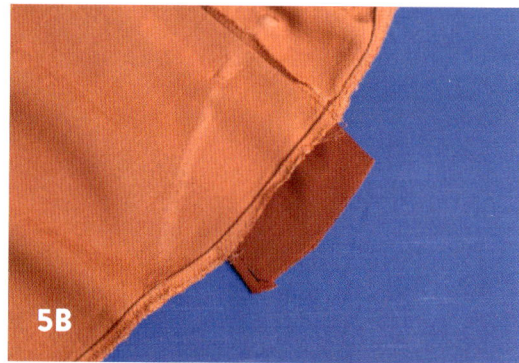

5B

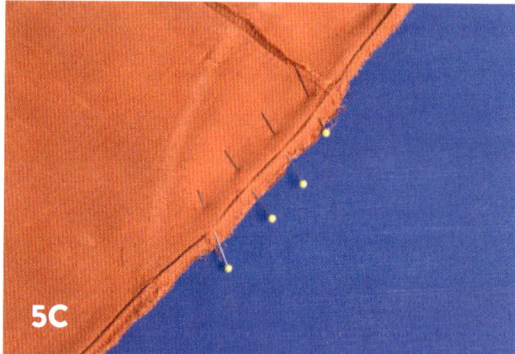

5C

Line up the edge of the tie with the edge of the garment seam and pin it in place. On your sewing machine, select a short straight stitch. We're going to sew the seam closed following the exact stitch line we just ripped, just with the tie inside this time. Start stitching along the last inch (2.5 cm) of the garment's seam allowance, backstitching at the beginning. This helps us keep the garment seam from unraveling now that it's been seam ripped. Continue sewing along the seam, finishing about an inch (2.5 cm) below the tie with a backstitch. All that's left is to finish your seam allowance with a zigzag stitch or overlocker, again starting and ending an inch beyond your tie.

You're all done! Go put on your garment, wait for someone to ask if you're free, and respond, "Sorry, I'm all tied up!" But maybe test that line first on someone whose friendship you don't mind losing.

5D

5E

We're Busting Outta Here

Upsizing clothing is near and dear to my heart. By age 14, I had DD boobs, which meant clothes shopping was pure hell. It primarily consisted of going to Kohl's® with my mom, trying on everything in the teen section, crying because none of it fit, and then being forced to shop from the women's section—then crying even more because everything looked so matronly on me. The clothes in my closet weren't things I liked wearing; they were just the few items I could find that fit my chest.

To remedy all of this, my mom became my alterations specialist, taking dresses two sizes too large in everywhere but my chest to fit the rest of me. From that young age, I knew alterations were going to be a staple in my life.

If any of this sounds familiar, it's time to meet your new best friend: upsizing. In this chapter, we'll tackle gaping button-down tops, shorts that fit like sausage casings, and jeans that just don't want to fit you anymore.

Needing to upsize your clothing instead of just finding clothes that fit can be infuriating. But so many of us are in this boat because brands refuse to create clothes that fit our boobs, hips, thighs, stomachs, etc., so I want to make this process as enjoyable as possible for you! This is your chance to completely customize your clothing. Gone will be your days of hunting for the one item that fits your body and maybe half fits your style. It's your turn to be the trendsetter who gets to coyly tuck your hair behind your ear and say, "Thanks, it's one of a kind."

Mind the (Button) Gap

Oh, the button-down shirt. It will be a part of our lives forever—from school to work uniforms and everywhere in between. The button-down is a staple, but if you're like me, it's a staple that's barely keeping its grip on the stack of paper that is your chest. If you've ever had a friend frantically mouth "your button" at you right before you notice your bra is out on show for the world, this hack is for you.

LEVEL
Beginner

SUGGESTED FABRIC
Any button-down, any fabric (but you know I'm going to suggest it be a woven fabric).

MATERIALS
Button-down garment

Pins

Matching thread

Sewing machine

Zipper foot or edgestitching foot

> **Heads-up:** If ever there was a project where your thread should perfectly match your garment, it's this one!

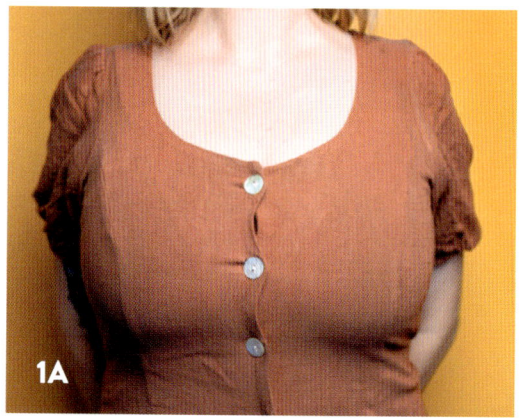

1A

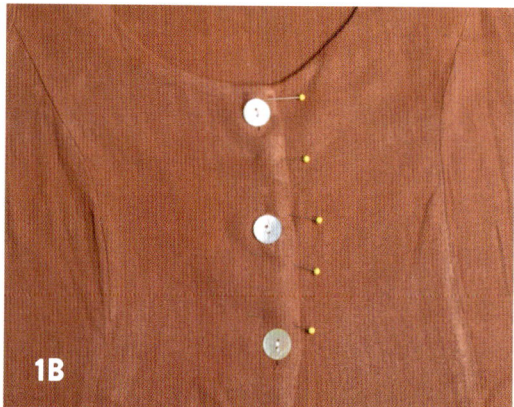

1B

Once you've closed the necessary buttons, lay your garment with the placket (the part of your garment with the buttonholes) perfectly flat. Pin the edges of the placket in place, only between the buttons that are going to remain permanently closed.

Step 2: Attach Your Zipper Foot

Time to pick the right presser foot. You can use a zipper foot or an edgestitching foot. Your machine most likely comes with a zipper foot, so this will be our focus. A zipper foot is designed to allow your needle to sew as close as possible to a zipper, but in this instance, we're using it to sew as close as possible to our buttons. Your standard presser foot has about ¼ inch (6.5 mm) of steel on each side of the needle. A zipper foot, on the other hand (or foot), can be placed entirely on the right or left of your needle, leaving the needle free to get as close as possible to its target.

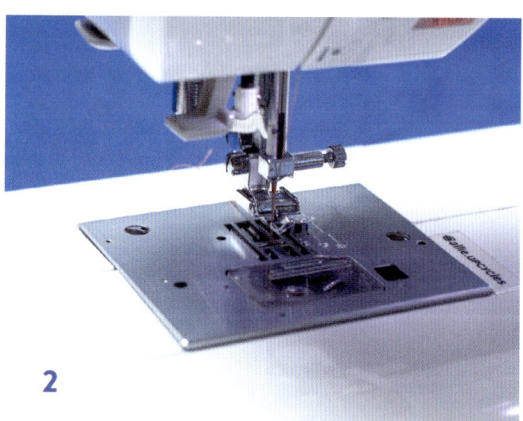

2

Step 1: Close the Buttons That Run Along Your Chest

Put on your button-down garment and close just the buttons over your chest, otherwise known as The Troublemakers. With only these buttons closed, take the garment off over your head to make sure your head doesn't get stuck. Then try pulling the garment back on, making sure you can still slide the bottom half of the garment over your chest. If the garment gets stuck, see if you can undo just one button at the top or bottom of your chest. Your chest is often the part of your torso that sticks out the farthest, so I don't expect you'll have an issue.

110 • NOT YOUR GRAN'S SEWING BOOK

If you've never changed a presser foot before, don't panic! It's very simple. Just head back to Presser Feet (page 29) for the lowdown. If you're sewing a "female" garment, attach the zipper foot on the right side of the needle, and vice versa if you're sewing a "male" garment. Of course, clothing doesn't have gender, but because of outdated historical practices when women were dressed by others, buttons are placed on different sides depending on what sex the garment was designed for. And thus, zipper foot placement matters.

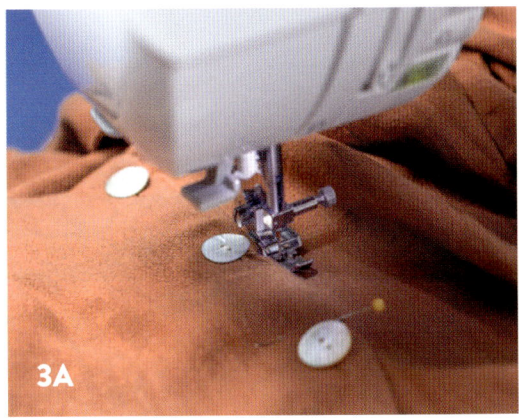

Step 3: Edgestitch the Placket Closed

With the chest buttons closed, take the garment to the sewing machine. When you lay your garment down on your machine, the top of the garment should be facing up. If you're sewing a female-designed garment, the placket will open on the right when it's laying down like this and vice versa for a male-designed garment.

Position your needle on the edge of the placket in line with the center of the first closed button. Using a straight stitch and a medium–long stitch length, sew from your first closed button down to your last closed button, backstitching at the beginning and end. If your placket has a line of straight stitching along the edge already, perfect! Just sew over this line. If it doesn't, just sew as close to the edge as possible.

And that's it! Once you're finished sewing, throw on your garment and marvel at the fact you can't see through to your bra. Buttons 0—Boobs 1.

Hips & Thighs Don't Lie

As Shakira told us, "Hips don't lie," and unfortunately, they don't always fit in off-the-rack clothing either. Same goes for my fellow thick-thighs-save-lives advocates. If you've been blessed with some extra junk in the trunk, hips, or thighs, you're used to the bottom of your shorts, dresses, and long shirts feeling more restrictive than a juice cleanse. It's time to give that hot bod of yours some breathing room by adding slits to those too-tight clothes. You can also use this same method to create decorative slits in other garments like skirts or sleeves.

For this project, we're utilizing facing. Facing is used to conceal raw edges, like a fancier version of a hem. Instead of folding the edges over twice and sewing them in place, facing is a completely separate piece of fabric that encloses the raw edge. It's the go-to method to create any type of cutout in your clothes.

LEVEL
Intermediate

SUGGESTED FABRIC
Your garment should preferably have side seams. Grab scrap fabric that is similar to your garment in color and type. For the easiest time sewing, err on the sturdier side for your scrap fabric. The fabric only needs to be 2½ inches (6.4 cm) wide. You'll figure out how long it needs to be in Step 1.

MATERIALS
Any garment where the hem is too tight
Pins
Chalk or washable marker
Ruler or measuring tape
Facing fabric
Seam ripper
Scissors
Thread
Sewing machine
Iron

Heads-up: This tutorial is designed for a garment where the top half fits fine but the bottom half can't contain your curves. If your garment fits just fine at the bottom once it's on but you struggle to pull it on over all your curves, head on down to Zipper-ty-Doo-Dah (page 119).

Step 1: Measure and Cut Your Facing

First up, we need to determine how long of a slit we need to create and how much facing we'll need to do that.

Try on your too-tight garment right side out and use a pin or some chalk to mark where it starts getting tight. Ideally this will be on a side seam, but if you have a seamless garment, you can choose your own adventure as to where your new slit(s) will be.

Now take the garment off and measure from the bottom hem of the garment up to your too-tight mark, then add 1¾ inches (4.5 cm) to that measurement:

Distance from bottom of garment to too-tight mark + 1¾ inches (4.5 cm)

This will be the length of your facing fabric. This width of your facing fabric will be 2½ inches (6.4 cm). (I've officially done the math for you one time, so you can't get upset with me for having to do math at any other point in this book.)

For each slit you're creating, grab a piece of fabric that's at least this long and wide and is similar in color and fabric type to your garment. If you don't have an exact match for the fabric type, err on the side of a stiffer fabric. We want a decent color match because this fabric will be a little bit visible when you move around in the garment, kind of like a zit you've

covered perfectly with your bangs until a gust of wind comes (but hopefully you think the inside of your garment is cuter than a zit).

On the fabric, draw a rectangle that is 2½ inches (6.4 cm) wide and your calculated length. Cut out one fabric rectangle for every slit you're creating.

Step 2: Finish the Rectangle's Edges

Now for a bit of boring work (I say as if cutting rectangles is riveting fun)—let's finish the edges of this rectangle. If you're dedicated to always cleanly finishing your raw edges (please tell me what being put together feels like), hem all four edges of your rectangle by folding in each side ⅜ inch (1 cm). After you've folded in all the edges, fold just the bottom edge over another ⅜ inch (1 cm). Iron and sew your hems in place (see Hemming & Hawing, page 44).

If you own a serger and are lazy like me, just serge around all three sides except the bottom edge. We are still going to hem the bottom edge of the rectangle (yeah, I know you thought you could get out of it)—fold up ⅜ inch (1 cm) of fabric, then fold the fabric over another ⅜ inch (1 cm). Iron and sew your bottom hem in place.

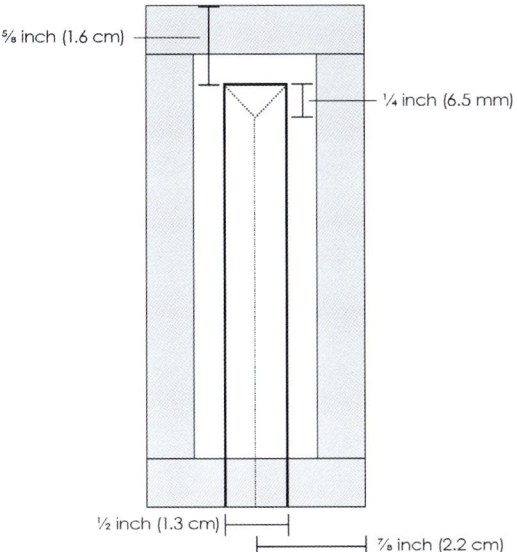

Diagram of your stitching lines.

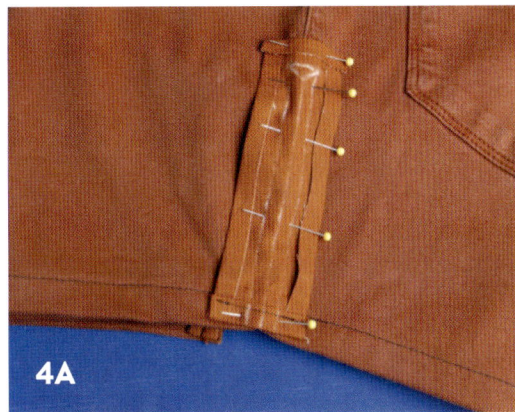

Step 3: Draw Your Stitching Lines

Take your now hemmed rectangle, or facing, and lay it right side down so all the folds are visible. In the middle of our facing, we're going to draw a ½-inch (1.3-cm)-wide rectangle that begins at the bottom hem and ends ⅝ inch (1.6 cm) below the top of the facing.

At the very bottom of your facing, mark the horizontal center, which is ⅞ inch (2.2 cm) in from either side. At ⅝ inch (1.6 cm) below the top of your facing, mark the horizontal center again. Draw a straight line connecting these two marks so they can meet up and each say, "Oh hi, Mark." This line is the center of your facing as well as the line that will match up with your garment's seam.

Now let's draw the ½-inch (1.3-cm)-wide rectangle around this line. Draw a straight line ¼ inch (6.5 mm) to each side of the center line, again ending ⅝ inch (1.6 cm) below the top of your facing. Connect these two lines at the top.

Finally, measure ¼ inch (6.5 mm) down from the top of your center line and draw a little mark. Draw a straight line from this mark to each of the rectangle's top corners to make a little triangle.

Whew, that was a lot of measuring. Take a breath, forgive me, and let's move forward to the fun part: sewing!

Step 4: Pin and Sew Your Facing to Your Garment

Lay your garment down right side up and lay your facing on top of it right side down so the right sides are touching. Line up the hem of your garment with the bottom hem of your facing, and line up your garment's seam with the center line of the facing. Pin your pieces together around the perimeter of your facing.

At last, let's sew the rectangle we just painstakingly measured and drew! Well, really it's more of a peninsula because we didn't draw a line at the bottom. Using a short–medium straight stitch, begin stitching from the bottom hem and sew along the peninsula you drew, backstitching at the beginning and end.

When you get to each corner of your rectangle, there's no need to remove your garment, cut the thread, and start stitching again on the next side. Instead, when you reach a corner, place your needle in the down position so it's holding your fabric in place. Then lift your presser foot, rotate your fabric 90 degrees so your next line is directly in front of your needle, lower your presser foot, and keep stitching.

Step 5: Cut Your Slit

Finally, my favorite part—cutting it all up (does this say something about me being a destructive person? Nah, surely not). Following your facing's center line/your garment's seam with your scissors, cut through both layers of fabric and STOP ¼ inch (6.5 mm) before you get to the top of your stitched rectangle (that's why we drew a little mark there). If your garment has some bulky overlocked seam allowance left over on either side of your cut, go ahead and trim that off.

Now we're making two angled cuts. From the very top of your vertical cut, cut to each top corner of your stitched rectangle, snipping as far into each stitched corner as you can without cutting the stitches. (If you do accidentally cut through them, you're in great company. Many a time have I had to go back and restitch the stitches I accidentally snipped).

5

Your stitched rectangle should now be sliced up into two symmetrical trapezoids on the left and right and a triangle at the top.

Step 6: Fold, Iron, and Sew Your Facing

This is where the magic happens. We're about to transform these weird cut-up shapes into a cleanly finished slit. Fold the top and sides of your facing to the inside of your garment by way of the cut you just made. Would you look at that? You now have a ½-inch (1.3-cm)-wide opening in your garment with beautifully finished edges. As someone who used to just slice open all of my clothes with no regard for the raw edges, I feel like a prize-winning architect when I look at the clean lines I create with facing.

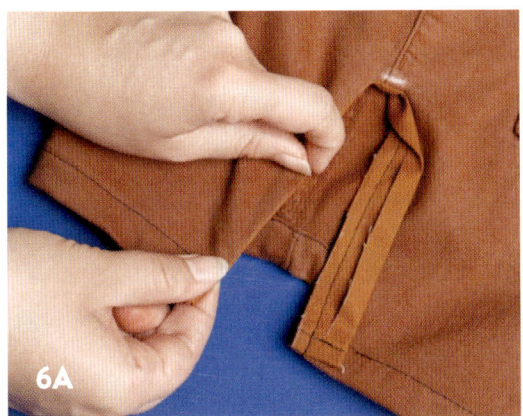

6A

6B

6C

On the inside of your garment, you'll see that the trapezoids and triangle we cut are tucked underneath the finished hem of your facing. Use an iron to press your facing on the inside of your garment to make the slit's seams even sharper.

Finally, let's sew one last rectangle (peninsula). We're going to topstitch around the three sides of our new opening to keep the facing in place and any raw edges hidden. With your garment right side up, use a medium straight stitch to sew a rectangular peninsula around the three sides of your opening, stitching ¼ inch (6.5 mm) in from the seam. As always, backstitch at the beginning and end.

Give everything a final press with your iron, and voilà—we're finished! With one side at least. If you're replicating this on the other side of your garment, finish that up and come back. I'll hold the celebration just for you.

Now enjoy the freedom that is letting your hips and thighs breathe again in your perfectly finished slits!

Zipper-ty-Doo-Dah

I can distinctly recall the terrifying time I got stuck in a shirt while alone in a Plato's Closet® dressing room at age 16. My pickings were slim at teen-focused consignment stores, so I had to try on anything that had even the slightest potential of fitting. After throwing a Hail Mary and forcing on a shirt that I knew would look cute if I could just get it over my chest, the panic set in. I realized I could not get the shirt back off. I wondered what would be written on my tombstone after I died of embarrassment in that changing room.

After much heavy breathing, sweating, a couple of tears, and squishing my boobs every way imaginable, I managed to free myself from the top with the sound of only a few snapped threads ringing in my ears. I vowed never to get myself into that situation again.

If only 16-year-old me knew how to install zippers in her clothing. Adding a zipper to an existing seam is an absolute game changer. This project is designed to help those with large chests put on a top that's tight in the waist and stomach and those with wide hips who struggle to pull on form-fitting skirts and dresses.

LEVEL
Advanced

SUGGESTED FABRIC
You'll need a garment that you fear you won't be able to get out of once it's on. We're adding a zipper to this, which is about 15 times easier to do on a woven fabric. If your garment is knit, you *must* use woven or nonwoven interfacing along the seams to prevent pain and punishment of epic proportions. As for the zipper, we'll learn all about them in Step 3, so get excited!

MATERIALS

Garment that reaches an impasse when you pull it on your body

Seam ripper

Thread

Sewing machine

Chalk or washable marker

Pins

Interfacing (optional)

Iron

Zipper

Zipper foot

Scissors

> **Heads-up:** This tutorial is designed for a garment that fits just fine at the bottom once it's on, but you struggle to pull it on over all your curves. If the top half fits fine but it can't contain your curves on the bottom half (a.k.a. you're blessed with wide hips or thick thighs), head back to Hips & Thighs Don't Lie (page 113).

Step 1: Seam Rip Your Garment Open and Sew the Hem

Pick the seam where you'd like to add your zipper (I suggest a side seam) and seam rip it open (see Let 'Er Rip, page 35). You'll need to rip open both the seam and any overlocking stitches holding the seam together. Normally I'd tell you to try on a garment to determine how large of an opening you'd like, but I fear that once you try this garment on, you won't be able to take it off.

1A

If you're opening a side seam on a shirt, a safe bet is to open the seam from the bottom hem up to an inch below the armpit. Don't go all the way to the armpit, or you'll be walking around with the bottom of a zipper incessantly poking you like a 2010 Facebook poke war. If you're opening a seam on the bottom of a dress or skirt, open the seam from the bottom hem up to the widest part of the skirt or dress.

Even if you open the seam a bit wider than you intended, guess what? You can just sew the seam closed again! It's a much lower-stress situation than getting stuck in a garment inside a changing room.

The tricky-ish part of this seam ripping is the hem. To access the seam you're opening, you'll need to seam rip part of the garment's hem. Open the hem about 1½ inches (3.8 cm), with your seam in the center at the ¾ inch (1.9 cm) mark.

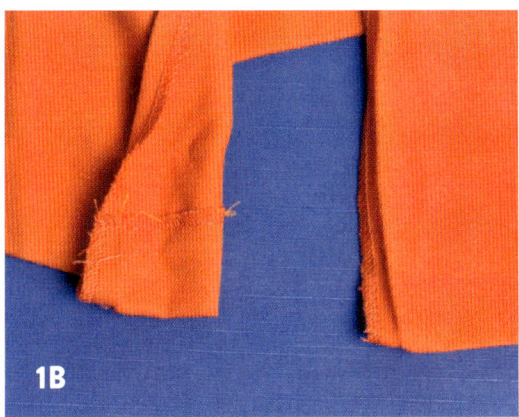

As soon as you've finished fully ripping your seam open, you can resew the hem on each side of the seam. Just fold the hem back up following the exact same folds already in the fabric, but make sure the side seam allowance you just opened remains *unfolded*. Pin the hem folds in place, select a medium–long straight stitch, and re-sew the hem. Make sure to backstitch on top of the last three stitches of thread where you seam ripped the hem; this ensures the thread doesn't come loose now that we've weakened it.

Once you've opened your seam and resewn your hems, try the garment on to make sure the opening is large enough to overcome the impasse of your curves. If you need a bit more wiggle room, just seam rip a bit higher!

After your seam is opened just right, mark the very top of this opening where your seam reconnects with some chalk or a washable marker. Draw these marks on each side of the seam allowance. Now rip your seam open another ½ inch (1.3 cm) or so. This extra space will better allow us to reach the very end of the zipper with our machine later.

Finally, if you had to seam rip the overlocking stitches that finished the edge of your seam allowance, it's time to redo all you've undone (I say as if it's your fault that you followed my instructions). Using a zigzag stitch or overlocker, finish the edges of both seam-ripped seam allowances (see Finishing Seams, page 32).

Step 2 (Optional): Iron Interfacing to Your Seam Allowance

This step is optional if your garment is made from a woven, sturdy fabric. If your fabric is stretchy or lightweight (like linen), this step is nonnegotiable—like exclaiming "Horses!" when you drive past a field of horses.

I can't tell you how many times a wonky zipper has made me cry and doubt all my sewing abilities. The reality is that even an advanced sewist will struggle to attach a zipper to stretchy fabric if they haven't prepped it correctly. Zipper tape (which I'll tell you more about in Step 3) is fairly stiff, so we need our garment's seam allowance to match.

Grab some sturdy iron-on interfacing and cut two pieces that are the length (plus 1 inch [2.5 cm]) and width of your open seam allowance. Following the instructions for your specific interfacing, iron one piece onto each of your seam allowances. It doesn't matter if the interfacing is on the right or wrong side of your seam allowance. For more information on interfacing and how to attach it, head back to The (Fabric) Choice Is Yours (page 20).

Step 3: Select Your Zipper

Once you're happy with your seam opening, measure the distance from the bottom of the hem to the mark you made at the top of your seam opening in Step 1. This measurement will be the length of the zipper you need to buy (or otherwise acquire; I don't need to know your methods).

When shopping for a zipper, select the one that is advertised as being the exact length of your measurement. For example, if you measure 10 inches (26 cm), you need to buy a zipper that is labeled as being 10 inches (26 cm). The total length of the entire zipper will actually be closer to 12 inches (31 cm). This is because a zipper is made up of the zipper teeth and the zipper tape. The zipper tape is the fabric on either side of the teeth that we sew directly onto the garment, and it typically extends around 1 inch (2.5 cm) above and below the zipper teeth.

Select a zipper that is the same color as your garment. If it's a patterned garment, lucky you! You have a range of colors to choose from! It's important to decide how visible you want your zipper to be. Do you want it to become a design element, or do you want to keep your zipper a secret? To make the zipper a design element, consider a metal or chunky plastic zipper. If you want to keep things hush hush, use a nylon coil zipper. The most hidden zipper of all is an invisible zipper, but these are built differently and are super tricky to sew, so we're going to forgo them here. A nylon coil zipper will be hardly visible, and it's easier to sew than an invisible zipper.

Step 3.5: Have a Snack

You've just returned from the sewing supply store with your zipper, so make sure you've washed your hands, had a glass of water, and eaten a snack before carrying on with any zipper sewing. Zipper sewing can be finicky, so it's crucial you eliminate any risk of getting hangry during the process.

Step 4: Attach One Side of the Zipper to the Open Seam

Now let's zip through the rest of this project! (Pause for eruption of laughter.) I always find it confusing figuring out which side of the zipper should be on which side of the garment, so take my hand and trust the process as I guide you through this. One thing to note: When I refer to the right side of a zipper, I mean the side that the pull tab is on.

Place your garment right side up on a flat surface with the hem at the top. Unfold your seam allowance so it's fully visible. Lay your zipper right side down, lining up the right edge of your zipper tape with the edge of the seam allowance on the *left* side of the seam opening.

I know this looks and sounds incorrect, but it all has to do with the fact that the seam allowance is currently unfolded, so just keep trusting me.

Now that you understand how the zipper should be positioned, you can unzip it. We'll be continuing to focus on the right half of the zipper and the left side of the open seam.

Line up the very top of the zipper teeth with the folded edge of your hem. There will be extra zipper tape dangling off the edge. The zipper teeth should be facing toward the left, and the edge of the teeth should line up with the fold where the seam allowance used to be pressed under.

Starting from the top, pin this side of the zipper in place. I find it easiest to pin vertically along the zipper tape, with the sharp bit of the pin facing toward the top. When pinning the top of the zipper in place, fold the overhanging zipper tape back so it's not visible beyond the hem of your garment. You'll need to angle this extra tape out slightly so it's not folded directly onto the zipper teeth.

Step 5: Sew One Side of the Zipper in Place

Off to the sewing machine! The zipper tape should be facing up, and we will start sewing from the garment's hem. Before we go any further, it's time to attach the zipper foot (see Presser Feet, page 29)! Because our zipper teeth are facing left, we need to attach the foot to the right of the needle.

With a medium straight stitch and your needle centered, line up the left side of your presser foot with the inside edge of the zipper teeth. I recommend using your machine's handwheel to slowly insert your needle into your tape. This way you can make sure the needle is going into the zipper tape directly to the side of your zipper teeth and not sewing into the zipper teeth. If you sew directly into the zipper teeth, you are literally in for a bumpy ride that will end in your zipper pull getting stuck on thread.

Once you're confident your needle is in the correct place, use your pedal to continue slowly stitching along your zipper, making sure to hug the inside edge of the teeth like James Bond scaling the side of a building on a narrow ledge.

As your stitching nears the end of the zipper teeth, you will need to move your zipper pull to finish sewing down this side. Some people are really talented at moving the pull without interrupting their sewing. I call this witchcraft. To make your own magic, make sure your needle is down, holding your garment in place. Lift your presser foot and pull the zipper tab up past your needle, turning your fabric a bit if you need to.

I personally find I can rarely fit my zipper pull past my presser foot. Instead, I sew as far as I can down my zipper then backstitch, cut my thread, and remove my garment from the machine. Then I pull the zipper tab up, return the garment to my machine like a mere mortal, and just restart sewing directly in front of where I've just backstitched. Be mindful to not backstitch over the same area twice, as we want to avoid creating too much bulk along the zipper.

Continue sewing a few stitch lengths beyond the end of your zipper teeth, then backstitch to finish. There will be about 1 inch (2.5 cm) of unattached zipper tape at the end—that is completely normal and will never get attached.

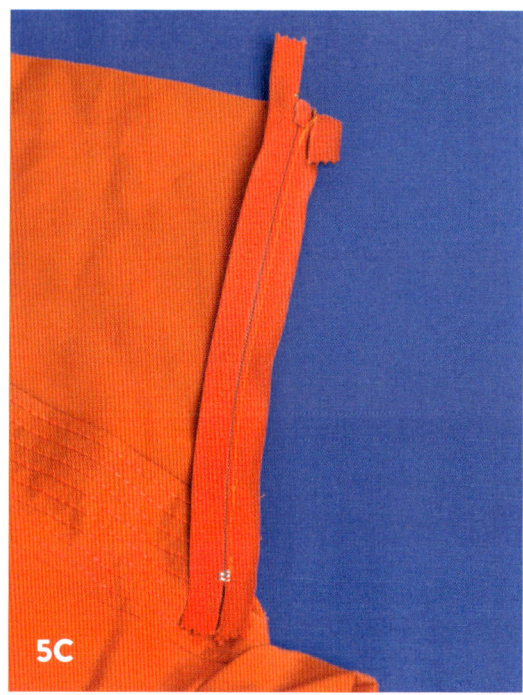

Step 6: Repeat Steps 4 & 5

Once more with feeling! We're going to repeat Steps 4 and 5 with the other side of the zipper, meaning you will need to mentally swap "left" and "right" in all the instructions.

You're probably asking how you're meant to pin the left half of your zipper to the right side of your open seam considering the direction your zipper is sewn. If you're not asking, I love and respect that confidence. Once again lay your garment down right side up with the hem at the top. Take the left half of the unzipped zipper, turn it one full rotation to the right, and lay it down on the seam allowance on the right side of the open seam. There will be a twist at the bottom of the zipper, but as soon as we fold both sides of the seam allowance back under at the end, the zipper will lay flat.

Now continue repeating Step 4. Once you're done pinning, zip your zipper closed. Your garment's hem on each side of your zipper *should* match up perfectly. If it doesn't, congratulations, you're just like me on 90 percent of my zipper projects. Just adjust and repin your zipper tape until it all matches up.

After you've perfectly pinned the second half of your zipper, repeat Step 5, ensuring you're swapping your zipper presser foot to the other side of the needle.

To more securely attach your zipper to your garment (which I absolutely think you should do unless you need to run out of the door in this garment this very second), you can sew the zipper tape to your seam allowance with a second line of stitching. Position your needle in the middle of your zipper tape and sew along the tape length using a short–medium straight stitch. It's always wise to have the safety net of an additional line of stitching for when you inevitably get fabric caught in your zipper one day and pull on it too hard in a state of hurry/fury.

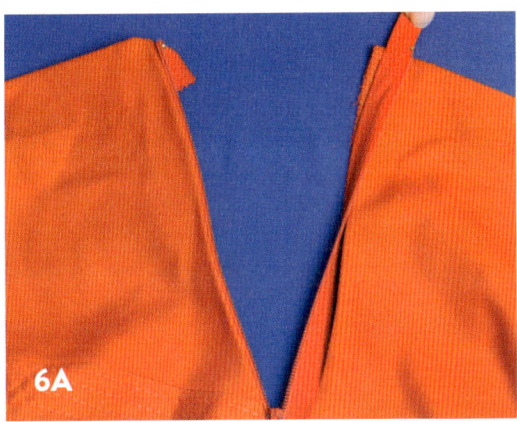

6A

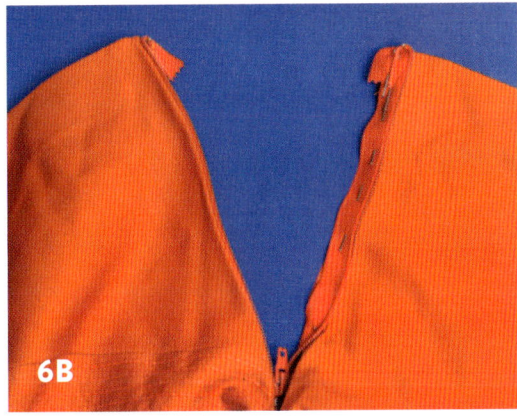

6B

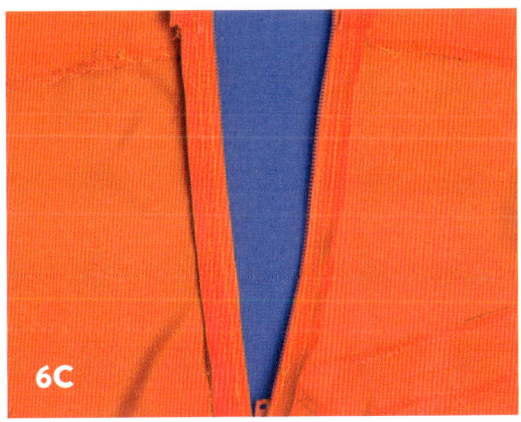

6C

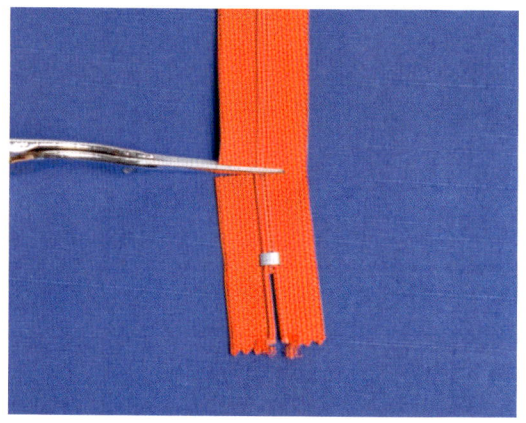

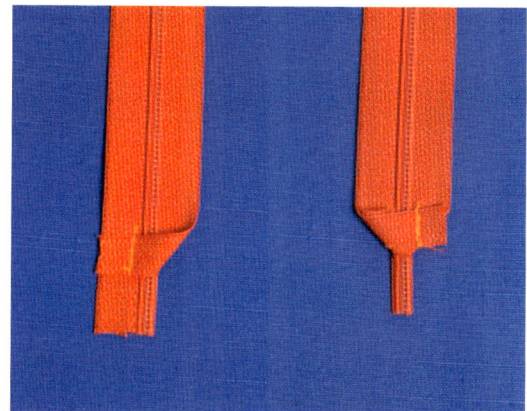

Oh hey!

If your zipper is significantly longer than the length of your open seam, let's shorten it! Cut off the remainder of the zipper 1 inch (2.5 cm) below where your zipper is sewn to the garment. Use non-fabric scissors for this bit so you don't damage them by cutting through the zipper teeth (even though this is something I'm absolutely guilty of).

Now we're going to cut the zipper tape away from the zipper teeth. Lining up your scissors with the outside edge of the zipper teeth, cut ½ inch (1.3 cm) up into the tape, directly to the right and left of the teeth. Take one of the flaps of zipper tape and fold it across the zipper teeth to the other side of the tape. Using a short–medium straight stitch, sew the flap to the opposite side of the tape. This does not have to be pretty. Just go over the flap a few times with your machine until you feel it's securely in place.

Repeat this process with the other zipper tape flap. You've now effectively built a wall of zipper tape that will function as a stop for the zipper pull. Go ahead and trim off the extra length of zipper teeth hanging below your tape.

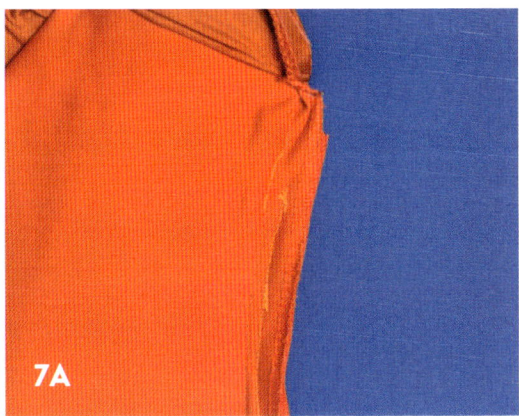

Step 7: Finish Your Seams

Once you've sewn your zipper on each side, zip it up and watch the magic of your seam allowances naturally folding back inside your garment. So satisfying.

At the very bottom of your zipper, we need to do a final short line of stitching. When you look at where your stitching on the bottom of your zipper tape ends and where the seam we opened is still stitched together, you should see a bit of unsewn no-man's-land in between. Our mission is to bridge that gap and visually blend the end of the zipper into the garment.

On your machine, place your zipper foot on the left side of your needle. Turn your garment inside out with the hem and zipper opening at the bottom, then close your zipper. Lay your garment on your machine so the zipper is laying on the right side of your needle, then line up your needle with the last ¼ inch (6.5 mm) of stitching on your garment's original seam.

With a medium straight stitch, backstitch, then sew along the last ¼ inch (6.5 mm) of your garment's original seam and continue sewing straight, following your garment's original seam exactly. These stitches will be parallel to those sewing your zipper in place,

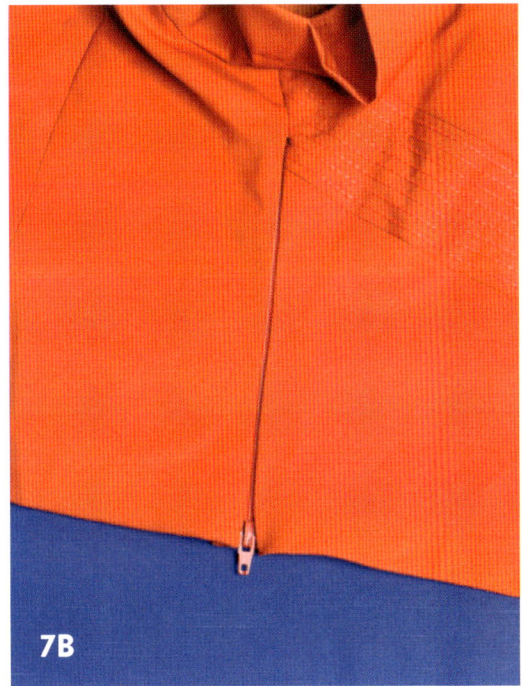

only a bit to the left. Once your needle is in line with the end of your zipper tape stitching (but sitting slightly to the left of it), sew three more stitches, then backstitch. Now your seam won't come undone, and the end of your zipper is tucked away in your garment!

Finally, best practice is always to give these folds a final press, *but be careful!* If you've used a plastic zipper, do not, I repeat, *do not* let your hot iron touch the zipper. Otherwise, you run the very real risk of melting the zipper teeth together, and you'll be right back where you started!

At last, unzip your zipper and slip into your garment with an ease you've never before experienced. Zip it closed around your curves with the confidence that you can get back out of this without fear, tears, or scissors.

Grow a Pair of Pants

Who hasn't had a too-small pair of pants taunting them from their closet? I remember how upset I was when I outgrew my favorite pair of jeans after a certain global event kept me confined to my tiny apartment for almost two years. I kept waiting for the day they would fit me again. After months of feeling down on myself, I decided to cut my losses—and the pants. I grabbed another pair of too-tight jeans and got to work combining the two. And wouldn't you know it, the new pair of pants I created was way cooler and drew in far more compliments than either of those old pairs.

Your body is going to change. That's pretty much nonnegotiable. When that happens, you can dwell on it or move forward. Personally, I'd rather we move forward together and make some really sick new pants for you.

LEVEL
Intermediate

SUGGESTED FABRIC
You'll need two pairs of pants or shorts, ideally made from a similar type of fabric, unless you're going for the dress/athletic pant look (which you genuinely might be, and if so, send pics of the final product!).

MATERIALS
Too-tight pair of pants or shorts
Additional pair of pants or shorts
Garment with waist size you like
Ruler or measuring tape
Scissors
Chalk or washable marker
Seam ripper
Pins
Thread
Sewing machine
Iron
Short piece of elastic

WE'RE BUSTING OUTTA HERE

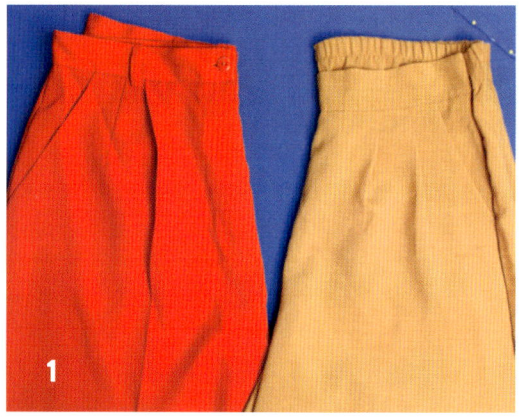 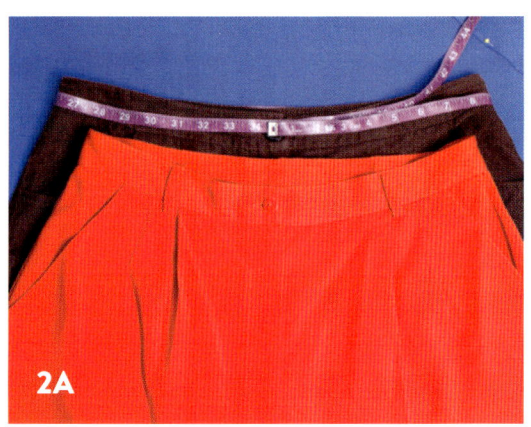

I'm using the red (left) as my primary pair of pants and the yellow (right) as my spare pair. The red pair has a waistband without a side seam, and the yellow pair has a waistband with a side seam. This will be important in future steps.

Step 1: Select Your Additional Pair of Pants

We're going to combine two pairs of pants that don't fit to make one single pair that does. It's easy to pick the main pair of pants you want to fix—these are the ones that shrank in the wash or that you always said would fit "one day" or that you bought before entering a healthy relationship with food. We will be using the entirety of this primary pair of pants. As for the secondary pair, we're just using it for spare parts (this project really has "heir and a spare" energy all over it). If you don't have a second pair of pants you're willing to sacrifice, I recommend heading to your local thrift store.

Remember when thrifting a second pair that you only need a few inches of these pants, so please avoid purchasing them in a size with limited options. Look for sizes that have ample pants available.

It's important that the spare pair of pants is the same length or longer than your primary pair, unless you plan to shorten the primary pair. Other than that, run wild with the color and pattern combination!

Step 2: Measure and Cut Your Additional Fabric

Let's first determine how much seam allowance we need for the additional fabric. Measure the seam allowance on your primary pants' side seam and jot this number down—we'll plug it into our formula in a moment.

The best way to figure out how much additional fabric you need to add to your pants is to grab a pair of pants or shorts that fits you perfectly. We're going to measure the waistband of this well-fitting pair as a guide, so it's important that the top of the waistband hits the same point on your body as your too-tight pants.

Close any flies or buttons on both pairs of pants. Use a measuring tape to measure around the circumference of your too-small waistband and then your just-right waistband. Subtract the smaller measurement from the larger, and what you're left with is the total amount of fabric you need to add to your pants. Divide this number by 2, add the seam allowance for a single seam, and you have the amount of fabric you need to add to each side of your pants.

Additional fabric for each leg:

$$\left(\frac{\text{circumference of just-right waistband} - \text{circumference of too-tight waistband}}{2} \right) + \text{seam allowance}$$

Take this measurement to your spare pair of pants. We're going to harvest our additional fabric along the side seam on the back pant legs. The front pant legs likely have pockets (or fake pockets, *booo*) along the side seam, and those will just get in the way. Line up a ruler or tape measure with the side seam, and measure and mark the width we calculated. Mark this measurement along the entire length of the back pant leg, then draw a line attaching all the marks together. With your sewing scissors, cut along this line from the hem through the waistband.

Repeat this on the second leg on your spare pants.

2B

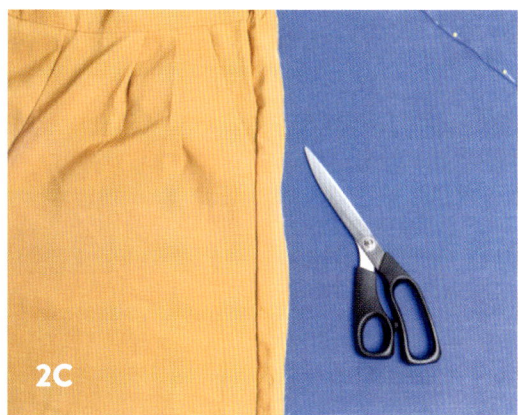

2C

Cut the line you drew starting from your hem and slicing all the way through your waistband.

Step 3: Seam Rip Both Pairs of Pants

Time to scrub in and get both pairs of pants ready for the transplant.

If you're lucky, both your pants' waistbands will have a side seam that lines up with the leg side seams. Unfortunately, it's more common that your waistband won't have a side seam at all. For all you unlucky ones, have no fear—I've included instructions for both types of waistbands. You can even combine one pair of pants with a seam-free waistband and one with a seam-full waistband. That's what I've done in this example to make all sides feel represented.

If you don't have a waistband side seam, first line up a ruler or straightedge with the top of each side seam on each pair of pants. With chalk or a washable marker, extend the seam line up through the top of the waistband. If your waistband has side seams, just keep on trucking (to the next paragraph—no marking necessary).

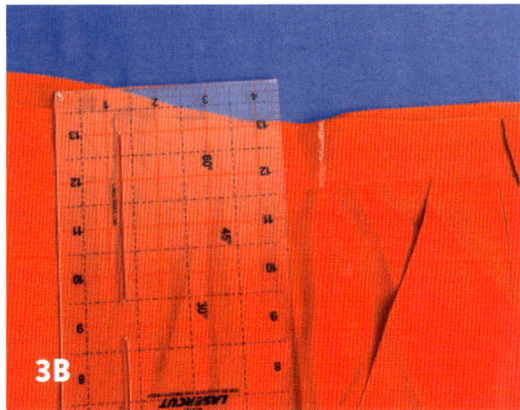

If your waistband does not have a side seam, line up a ruler with the pant leg seam and extend this line onto the waistband with some chalk.

It's time to let it rip. Seam rip the side seams of both pairs of pants. If your pants are hemmed, you'll need to seam rip the hem open at least an inch or two (2.5 or 5 cm) to access the end of the side seam. I personally recommend seam ripping the entire hem on your too-tight pair of pants so we can hem both parts of the pants all together at the end.

Once you reach the waistband, grab your scissors again—unless you have a side seam in your waistband, in which case just finish seam ripping up through the waistband (no no, none of us are envious of you at all). Before slicing straight through the waistband, it's helpful to seam rip the bottom edge a few stitches on either side of your legs' side seams. The very top of the seam allowance will be tucked under the waistband, and we want to free that from the waistband before cutting it. Once you've opened the band a bit, just wiggle the rest of the seam allowance out. *Now* you can cut straight through the line we drew on the waistband.

Repeat this waistband opening process on all four pant legs. You should be left with two long strips of fabric from the spare pants and one open pair of pants that could only stay on your body if you used suspenders.

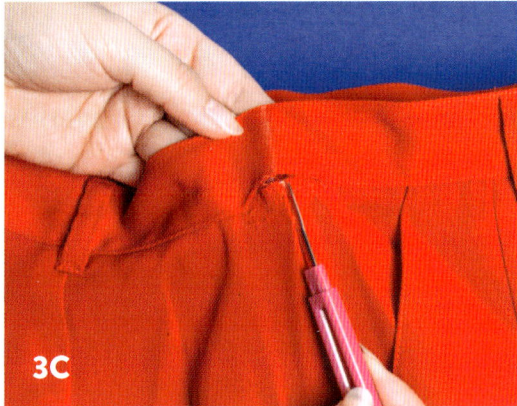

If your waistband does not have a side seam, seam rip the bottom of the waistband a bit and wriggle out the pant leg seam allowance.

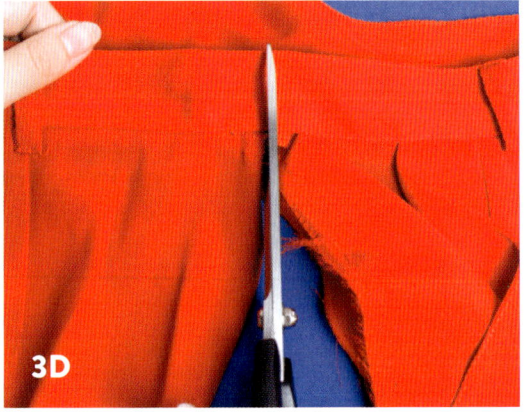

If your waistband does not have a side seam, cut straight through the waistband.

3.5A

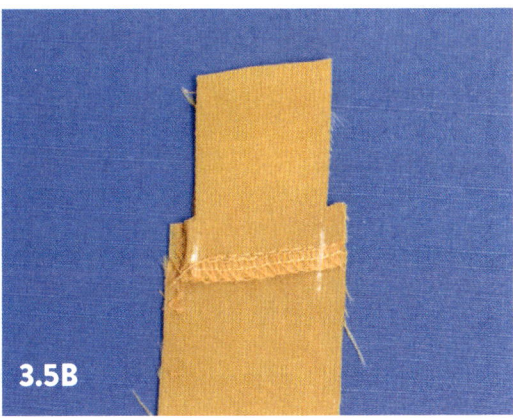

3.5B

Left: If your waistband did not have a side seam, the leg seam allowance extends beyond the end of the waistband. Right: If your waistband did have a side seam, all the edges line up.

A portion of the waistband removed so we can match up seam allowances with those from a side-seamless waistband.

Step 3.5: Remove a Small Piece of the Waistband (Side-Seamless Waistbands Only)

If your waistband didn't have a side seam, you'll notice after cutting and seam ripping that the leg side seams extend further than the waistband. Meanwhile, the edge of the waistband and the leg side seam line up perfectly on the spare fabric that we cut from hem to waistband. The same will also be true if your waistband had a side seam. (As you can see in the photo above, my red pants didn't have a waistband seam, and my yellow pants did).

While people can come in all shapes and sizes, we really need our side seams and waistbands to be uniform. Where the seam allowance and waistband line up perfectly, we need to remove the very end of the waistband to allow the seam allowance to extend beyond it. For example, if your seam allowance is ½ inch (1.3 cm), you need to remove the final ½ inch (1.3 cm) of the waistband.

Measuring from the end of the spare fabric's waistband, mark the seam allowance measurement from Step 2. Seam rip the bottom of the waistband from the raw edge to this mark, then cut off the excess waistband fabric at the seam allowance mark.

Now all four seam allowances extend beyond the cut edge of the waistband.

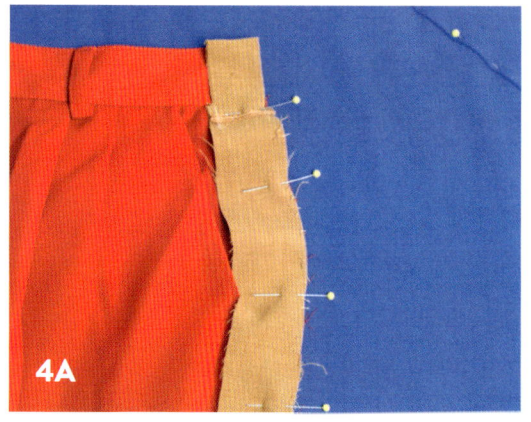

Step 4: Attach the Spare Fabric to the Too-Tight Pants

Turn your too-tight pants inside out and grab your spare fabric strips. As you may have suspected, the fabric strip from the left leg of your spare pants should be added to the left leg of your too-tight pants, and same for the right leg.

With the right sides touching, match up your too-tight pants' side seam allowance with the spare fabric's seam allowance and pin them together along the entire seam. When you're working on the seam that combines the existing seam allowances from both the too-tight and the spare pants, there's a chance these seam allowances are a different width. If this is the case, line up the folds where each seam was originally stitched together rather than the raw edge of the seam allowance.

If your pants both came with waistband side seams, continue pinning the seams together through the top of the waistband. If they didn't, I've got you. We have a whole separate step just for us! For now, just pin together the leg seam allowances and leave the waistband for later.

Finish your side seams or no dessert!

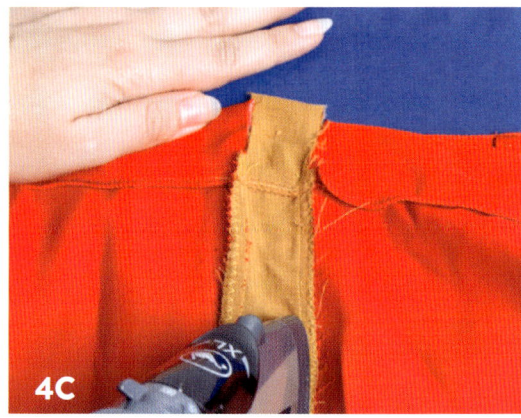

Press your side seams away from the spare fabric.

After you've pinned one seam, use a short–medium straight stitch to sew the entire seam, backstitching at the beginning and end. Finish the seam allowance with a zigzag or overlocking stitch (see Finishing Seams, page 32).

Repeat this process on all four side seams. I can feel you suddenly longing for the days when you thought pinning, sewing, and finishing just two side seams was a lot of work. And to that I say, "I hear you."

4.5A

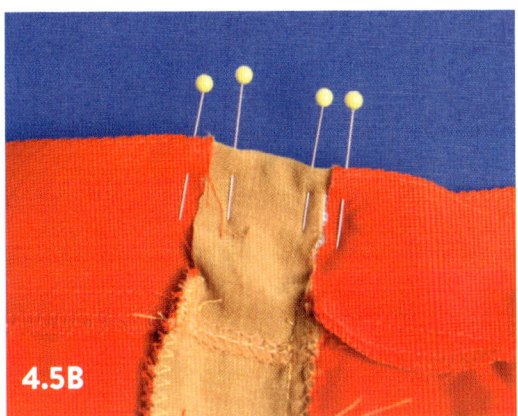

4.5B

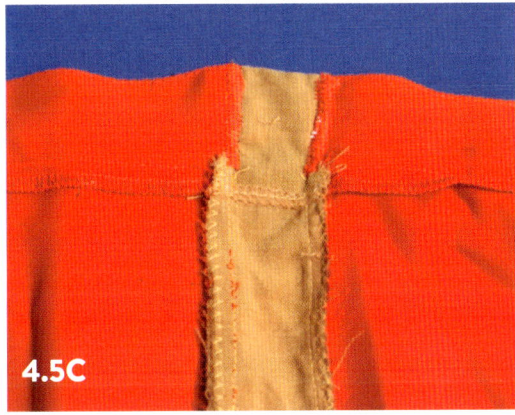

4.5C

Keep your garment inside out after finishing the seams and grab your iron. On each pant leg, fold both side seams away from the spare fabric and iron them in place. Make sure you keep these seam allowances facing outward when you finish your waistband (if you haven't already) and hem your pants.

If you were able to sew your waistband pieces together along the side seams in this step, you are free to skip to Step 5. The rest of us are going to go to this super-cool party at Step 4.5 though.

Step 4.5: Sew the Waistbands Together (Side-Seamless Waistbands Only)

Now to tackle this pesky waistband. We don't have any seam allowance to attach the waistbands, and that's usually what we rely on. Instead, we're going to get creative (in a sewing book? Revolutionary). We need to add another piece of fabric to the inside of our waistband to create an anchor for our stitches. I personally recommend using a piece of woven elastic. Alternatively, you could use some wide leftover ribbon that probably came wrapped around a seasonal bath set, or fold a piece of sturdy woven fabric in half.

4.5D

Whatever additional anchor fabric you select, it should be about ¼ inch (6.5 mm) narrower than your waistband and 1 inch (2.5 cm) longer than the spare fabric's waistband.

Slide the anchor fabric through the spare waistband, centering it vertically and leaving ½ inch (1.3 cm) hanging out on each open side. Place a pin through the center of the waistband to keep the anchor in place (anchoring the anchor, as it were). Slip the ½ inch (1.3 cm) ends of the anchor into the adjacent too-tight waistband openings.

Working on one seam at a time, push the raw waistband edges together so they kiss. Then pin through the too-tight waistband and anchor fabric to hold it all in place.

Before we sew both sides of the waistband together, make sure the top of the leg seam allowances are tucked inside the waistband.

Now to seal the deal. Select a zigzag stitch and a short stitch length. If you have multiple zigzag stitches, select the wider option. With each zig, the needle will sew one side of the waistband, and with each zag, it will sew the other. Back and forth until two waistbands become one—beautiful.

Starting at the top of the waistband, backstitch, then sew all the way down the waistband seam. When you reach the bottom of the waistband, press the reverse button on your machine and stitch backward all the way back up to the top, then backstitch (technically forward stitch since we were sewing backward). The short stitch length combined with two layers of zigzag stitching should make it impossible for this waistband seam to pull apart.

Repeat this process on all the waistband seams.

Finally, with a long straight stitch, we'll secure the bottom of the waistband in place since we weakened it with our seam ripping in Step 3. Starting and ending 1 inch (2.5 cm) outside the spare fabric waistband, edgestitch the bottom of the waistband, backstitching at the beginning and end.

Step 5: Topstitch the Seams (Optional) and Hem the Pants

Just like our two separate waistbands, it's great to have everyone back together for this final step. It's time to put the finishing touches on our new perfectly fitting pants.

If you would like, topstitch all the side seam allowances in place. This step isn't necessary, but it can help your side seams lay flat and is aesthetically pleasing. If you're into it, keep your garment right side out, select a medium-long straight stitch, and topstitch down each side seam. Make sure that your seam allowances are both still facing outward and keep your topstitching around ⅛ inch (3 mm) to the outside of the seam.

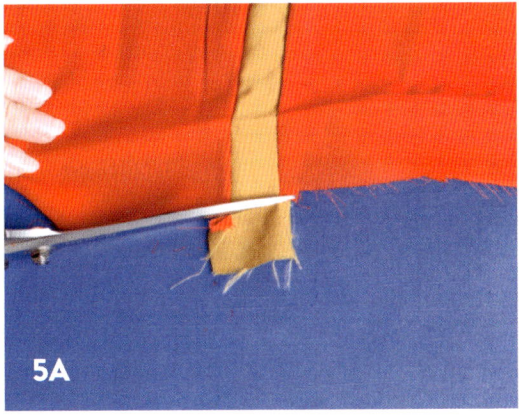

Let's finish strong and hem these Frankensteined pants. If the spare fabric is longer than the no-longer-too-tight pants, trim it now so it matches up with the raw edge of your unhemmed pants. Finally, fold, iron, and hem both pieces of the pants together as one cohesive unit (see Hemming & Hawing, page 44).

At last, you can wear these pants! No more hiding them in the back of your closet—it's time to take them for a spin in the real world. You now have a perfectly fitting, original pair of statement pants and plenty of scrap fabric that you can turn into pockets, ruffles, ties, or any other buzzwords from the project titles in this book!

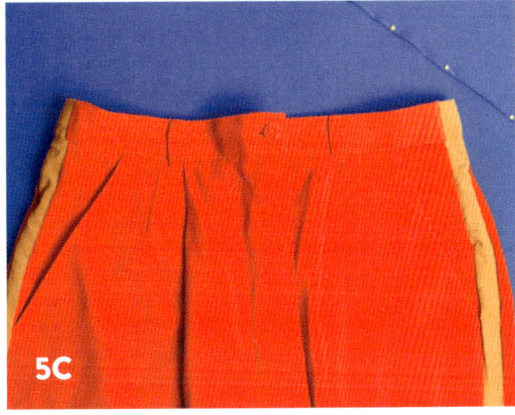

At last—ketchup and mustard in pants form.

Sleeves Please

There's something just so fun about giving a garment new sleeves. In my opinion, it's the best and easiest place to add personality to a top or dress.

I adore a color-block moment, so I typically replace sleeves on my garments to add a new color or two to my outfit. I also can't stand super-short sleeves (you'll learn a lot more about my vendetta against cap sleeves in this chapter), so I'm often looking for a way to lengthen them. Sometimes I achieve this by adding a ruffle at the bottom, and sometimes I just throw the whole sleeve out and create a new one (actually I save them for scrap fabric, but that doesn't sound as cool).

The appeal of adding new sleeves could be that you don't love your upper arms—yet; keep working on yourself, babe—you prefer more modest outfits, your muscles are too amazing, or clothing manufacturers just have not figured out how to make sleeves that don't suffocate your upper arms.

Fair warning: Of all the things you'll cut and sew, sleeves are probably the most confusing. But don't let that deter you! It's not terribly hard to sew sleeves, they just look weird because the opening of an armhole and the top of a sleeve are each curved in opposite directions. When you first try to figure out how these fit together, you might feel like a baby trying to force a triangular block into a circular hole. But just like you did as a baby, you'll figure this out too, especially if you read Replacing C(r)ap Sleeves (page 149).

Side Me Up: Shirt Gussets

Do you have a top you love but know you're one enthusiastic high five away from ripping off the arm? Do you try to hunch your shoulders and squeeze your arms in like a mischievous goblin to prevent your chest from popping out? If so, shirt gussets are about to be your best friend. These diamonds in the rough are added to your garment under and along your arms to give your chest and arms some much-needed breathing room (that diamond pun will make sense when you see the shape of a gusset). This tutorial is designed for tops that are uncomfortably tight in your armpits or around your upper arms or that pull across your chest (or all three if you're lucky!).

You don't have to stop at adding gussets to tops, though! Gussets are also ideal for bottoms that are too tight in the crotch and restrict everyone's everyday leg movements like squats and high kicks. In this tutorial I'll be focusing on shirt gussets, but if your pants are the problem, you can use all these same techniques to fix them.

LEVEL

Intermediate

SUGGESTED FABRIC

Your garment must have sleeves and side seams that run along the torso and underarm. Your gussets will likely be fairly small, so this is a great scrap-busting project! The gusset fabric should be the same type of fabric as your garment and ideally a matching color. If you want to choose a different color, might I suggest avoiding something that is almost identical but a couple shades darker? Otherwise, it will look a bit like you have permanently sweaty armpits (which, like, same).

MATERIALS

Garment with sleeves and seams

Seam ripper

Ruler or measuring tape

Paper

Scissors

Gusset fabric

Pins

Chalk or washable marker

Thread

Sewing machine

Iron

> **Heads-up:** Make sure you're repeating each step on your second sleeve as you go.

Step 1: Seam Rip Along the Underarm

Try on your too-tight top inside out. Make sure to button, zip, or otherwise close your garment the way you would normally wear it. You'll be able to see and feel where your top is pulling too tight. Use the pangs of pressure and discomfort to fuel you through this project.

Take your garment off and begin seam ripping in the armpit at the cross section where the sleeve and underarm/side seams meet. When I refer to the *sleeve seam*, I mean the seam that wraps over your shoulder and attaches your entire sleeve to the torso. When I refer to the *underarm seam*, I mean the straight seam that runs along the bottom of your sleeve from the armpit to the hem of the sleeve. The underarm seam eventually turns into the *side seam* on the garment's torso. If you were driving along the underarm seam, your GPS would

interrupt your music to tell you, "When you arrive at the sleeve seam, continue straight," and suddenly you've missed the beat drop and you're driving on the side seam.

As a jumping-off point, I recommend seam ripping the underarm seam 2 inches (5 cm) above the sleeve seam and the side seam 1 inch (2.5 cm) below the sleeve seam. This is of course assuming you haven't already accidentally ripped the underarm seams open with a single misplaced arm movement (don't worry; we've all done it).

Try your garment back on. If your pits are comfy and the chest isn't pulling, congrats, you're done seam ripping! If things are still too tight in places, take your garment off and continue seam ripping a bit at a time until you're comfortable.

Once your armpits are free and in the breeze, stop for a moment to consider the question "Could this be the new cold-shoulder top?"

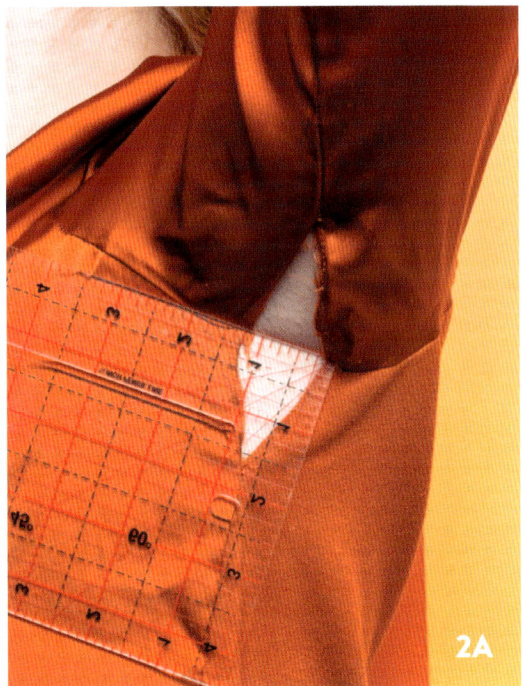

Step 2: Make Your Gusset Pattern

With your seam-ripped garment on, grab a ruler in your dominant hand and place your nondominant hand on your head. Now pat your head and rub your tummy. Kidding. Unless you want to. This act will reveal an open diamond shape that should resemble a kite in your armpit. The horizontal points of the kite are where your underarm/side seams meet the sleeve seam, and the vertical points are the ends of your seam ripping along the underarm and side seams.

Grab a ruler and measure the distance between the two horizontal points. Pay close attention to whether the kite's seam allowance has unfolded itself and is now visible. We're measuring from the points where the underarm/side seams were originally stitched together, not the raw edge of the seam allowance. Jot down this measurement and take your garment off.

Let's make our pattern! Grab a piece of paper like printer or notebook paper (you can of course use official pattern paper, but it's not necessary). In the center of the paper, draw a horizontal line that's the distance you've just measured. Draw a mark in the exact center of this line.

Now we need to measure the kite's vertical opening. Holding your open seam closed along the vertical line, measure the distance from the sleeve seam to the point your underarm seam reconnects. On your pattern, draw a vertical line this length up from the center of the horizontal line. Now repeat this process, this time measuring the distance from the sleeve seam allowance down to where the side seam reconnects. Draw a vertical line this length down from the center of the horizontal line.

Let's play connect the dots to make our kite. Using a straightedge, draw four diagonal lines to connect the adjacent tips of your cross.

2C

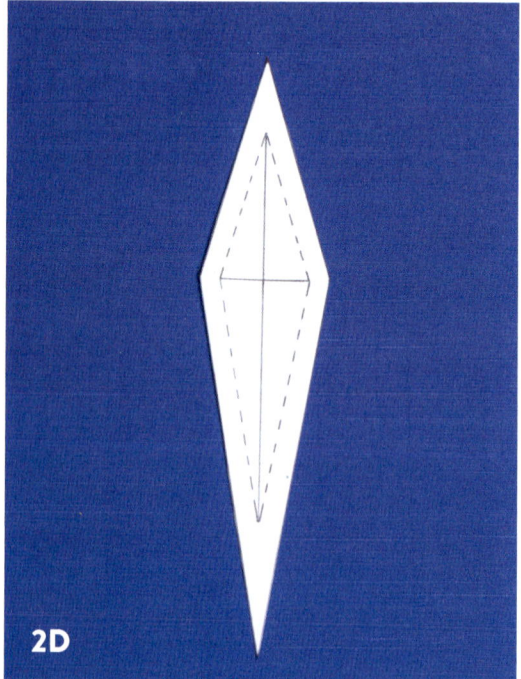

2D

A gusset pattern. The vertical line is the height of our sleeve opening, and the horizontal line is the width. The dotted lines are where we will sew our seams, and everything outside of these lines is the seam allowance.

Now we need to add seam allowance. Measure the width of your garment's seam allowance and add lines this distance to both ends of the horizontal line. Because of geometry and mathematical theories (I assume), we can't just add the same seam allowance to each end of our vertical line—it won't be long enough.

To avoid understanding the math myself, we're going to work around this. Line up the butt of a ruler with the outside of one of the four diagonal lines you drew. Measure and mark the seam allowance distance on two points along this line. Then, place your ruler through these two marks and the tip of the closest horizontal line, and draw a long straight line connecting them. Repeat this on all four sides of the diamonds. Make sure you draw these lines nice and long so they're able to intersect above and below your kite drawing. Now your seam allowances are all equal width and none of us had to learn geometry!

Cut out your paper kite along the four outside lines. Feel free to cut multiple in case you have a tiny animal that would look adorable in a photoshoot pretend-flying a kite.

Whew, that was a lot of measuring and drawing straight lines. I applaud you sticking it out. Things can only get more exciting from here!

Step 3: Prepare the Gussets

Grab your gusset fabric, fold it in half, and pin it together in a few places to keep it in position while you cut. Pin or trace your paper kite onto your fabric and cut through both fabric layers, creating two identical kites of fabric.

On the wrong side of both fabric kites, we're going to mark the seam allowance. I like to do this by laying my pattern on top of the fabric

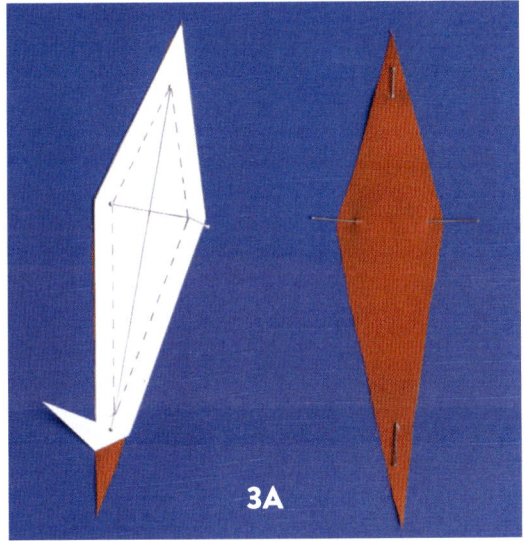

and grabbing four pins. Stick the pins in each of the four tips of the smaller kite drawing so they go through the paper and into the fabric. Then slowly remove the paper pattern, keeping the four pins in place, and voilà! You've marked the four points you'll need to match up with the open diamond on your garment.

Turn your garment inside out and grab one fabric kite (gusset). We'll use the pins we put in our gusset to pin it to the garment. With right sides touching, pin just one of your kite's horizontal points to one of your garment's horizontal points. The raw edge of your kite should line up with the raw edge of your garment's seam allowance. Make sure your kite is facing the correct direction so the length of the sides matches the length of the open seam.

Next, pin the vertical points on the gusset and garment together. Continue pinning the kite to your garment's seam along one side—underarm seam and side seam. I like to use different colored pins for the points to serve as a warning to my sewing machine not to dare sew past these points.

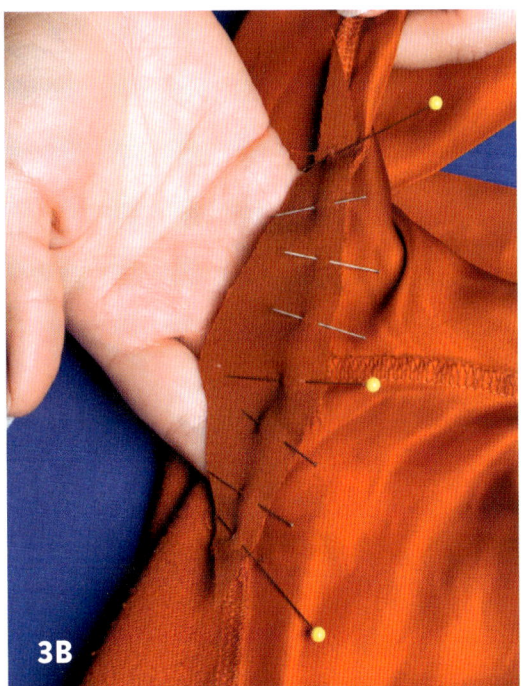

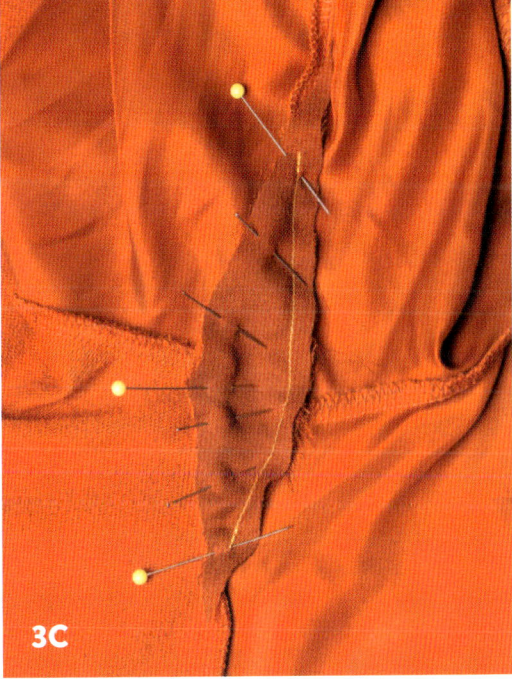

I used my long yellow pins to mark the sewing guides on the corners, and used smaller pins to hold the rest of the seam together.

SLEEVES PLEASE

Step 4: Sew the Gusset

Once you've finished pinning half of your gusset to your garment from vertical point to vertical point, we're off to the sewing machine! Select a short–medium straight stitch and line up your needle with the pin on the top point of your kite. Backstitch at the beginning, then continue sewing a straight line to the horizontal point, ensuring you're sewing at the seam allowance you measured in Step 3.

At the horizontal point, keep your needle through your fabric, lift your presser foot and turn your garment so you're ready to stitch straight down the next side. Lower your presser foot and continue sewing until you reach the pin at the bottom tip and backstitch.

Remove your garment from the machine so that we can pin and sew the next side of the gusset. Repeat the exact same process of pinning and sewing on the other half of the gusset.

Once all four sides of the gusset are sewn to the garment, finish the seams (Finishing Seams, page 32). If the vertical seam allowance on your gussets is a bit long, feel free to trim off any excess before finishing the seams.

5A

5B

Step 5: Restrengthen Your Garment's Seams

Let's ensure we haven't left any tiny open holes between the top and bottom of our gusset and the garment's original seams.

Flip your garment so the wrong side of your gusset is lying down on your sewing machine and your garment's side seam is facing up. Select a short–medium straight stitch. Line up your needle with the last ½ inch (1.3 cm) of stitching on your garment's original seam. This seam should be perfectly in line with the gusset's seam. Backstitch and sew along the garment's seam and continue sewing straight along the first ¼ inch (6.5 mm) of the gusset seam and backstitch. Repeat this process at the other end of the gusset.

At last, you can enjoy the comfort of wearing a top *and* having full range of motion in your arms—revolutionary! This garment is officially ready for you to stretch your arms above your head and go fly a kite.

Replacing C(r)ap Sleeves

Oh, cap sleeves. How you've made so many of our upper arms so uncomfortable. If you lived through the early 2000s, you felt the wrath of the cap sleeve. In the fight to end fashion waste, it can make things tricky when you're staring down the barrel of nothing but cap-sleeved shirts and dresses at the thrift store. As vindicated as many of us might feel seeing these all end up in the trash (incidentally the same way the sleeves made me feel at age 14), it's time for us to practice forgiveness and give these tops a second shot at life.

LEVEL
Intermediate

SUGGESTED FABRIC
Any garment with the dreaded cap sleeve! There's a good chance you're using a cap-sleeved T-shirt, so this may be your chance to finally try sewing knits. If you're worried about wonky seams, consider adding fusible woven, nonwoven, or knit interfacing along your seam allowance. For your new sleeves, you can go for broke with colors and patterns! I personally love contrasting sleeves, so this is a great chance to play with different colors and fabric finishes (shiny, matte, etc.); just make sure that if your shirt is woven, the sleeve is woven. Sleeves always take more fabric than you think, so for each sleeve, grab fabric around 1½ feet (0.5 m) wide and 1 foot (0.3 m) long.

MATERIALS
Cap-sleeved garment

Garment with a sleeve length you like

Seam ripper

Scissors

Chalk or washable marker

Pins

Iron

Ruler or measuring tape

Fabric of the same material as your garment

Thread

Sewing machine

SLEEVES PLEASE • 149

Step 1: Seam Rip the Sleeves off the Garment

Grab your cap-sleeved garment and a garment that has the sleeve length you'd prefer. Lay the cap-sleeved garment flat on top of the good-sleeved garment, matching up the armpit seams of the sleeves. Using the bottom seam of your sleeve as a guide, measure the distance from the bottom of your cap sleeve to the bottom of the good sleeve. Write this measurement down and save it for Step 2. Your good-sleeved garment has now served its purpose and can be returned to your closet/the chair that you pile all your clothes on.

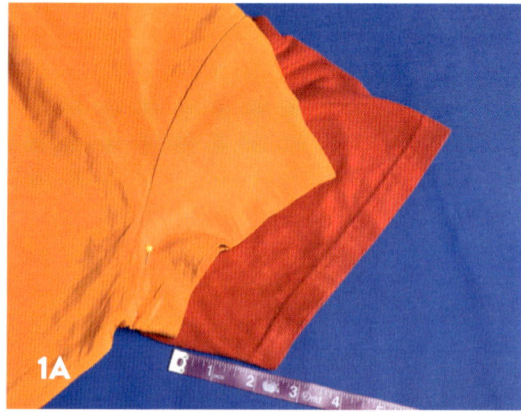

Now take your cap-sleeved garment, curse it one final time, and then let out a long breath as you release your anger toward it. All is about to be forgiven.

Grab your scissors and turn your garment inside out. We're going to snip the sleeve seam in three places to use as guides when we attach the new, better sleeve. Snip the seam allowances at the top of the sleeve and roughly halfway down each side. Make sure not to cut the seam itself.

Seam rip the cap sleeves off the torso (see Let 'Er Rip, page 35). We are going to use these original sleeves as a pattern, so it's important to resist all urges to mangle them and instead keep them fully intact. There are a couple different types of seams you'll encounter with cap sleeves. Some sleeves are first attached to the body of the garment with a straight stitch. Then the seam allowance is overlocked and topstitched into place. If this is the case for you, I recommend first seam ripping the topstitching, then the straight stitch, and finally the overlocking.

If the garment is a stretchy T-shirt, there's a good chance that the sleeve is attached to

the body of the garment exclusively with an overlocking stitch. You'll see this often with fast-fashion garments where the focus is quantity over quality. The silver lining is that it's quicker to undo, especially if the seam has already started unraveling itself as is wont to happen with fast fashion.

Once you've seam ripped the sleeve from the shirt, rip the underarm seam open as well so the sleeve can lay flat.

You may encounter a bit of a bird's nest where your torso side seam meets the sleeve seam. A sleeve is typically sewn by first finishing the seam around the shoulder opening, then sewing together the torso side seam and the underarm seam of the sleeve in one fell swoop. Seam rip the sleeve's underarm seam (which is typically all of ½ inch [1.3 cm] long on a cap sleeve).

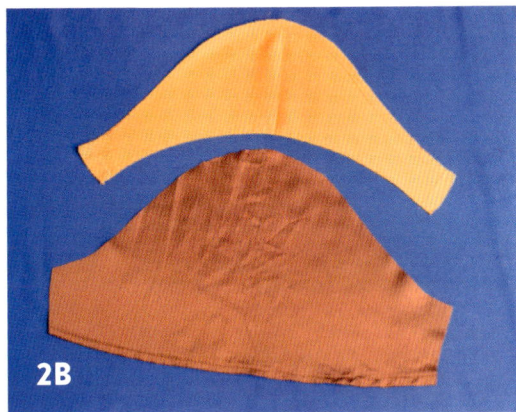

When you get to the point where that seam turns into the side seam of the torso, you may need to jump in there with some scissors and just snip the sleeve free from the side seams that bind it. Sometimes trying to seam rip that intersection of multiple seams can lead to more destruction than a little snip will.

Step 2: Cut Out Your New Sleeves

Once your sleeves are free, you'll probably feel a knot or two in your body free up as well. This is your body releasing its past resentment toward this garment.

Choose one of your cap sleeves to use as a pattern to create your new sleeves. I recommend marking with some chalk or pins which side of the sleeve attaches to the front of the shirt. The curve of a sleeve is slightly different in the front and back, and if you're like me, you always forget which is which when it comes time to attach sleeves.

I also recommend ironing your sleeve flat. In some cases, your sleeve's seams have been attached for years, so they're about as folded and creased as my back after an entire day of sewing. Before you iron it flat, make sure you measure the seam allowance of the underarm seam and jot this down. We'll need to replicate this seam allowance on the new sleeve in Step 3.

Grab the fabric you've chosen to become your new sleeves. Fold this fabric in half with the right sides touching so we can cut out both new sleeves at once. It's best practice to pin both sides together in a few places so it doesn't slip around while you're tracing and cutting. Place your now-flat cap sleeve on top of your fabric. With chalk or a marker, trace all sides of your cap sleeve except the bottom hem onto your fabric.

Next, we need to extend the length of the pattern so we can make the proper sleeve that your arms always deserved! Take your measurement from Step 1 and make sure to calculate any additional length you'll need to add to create your hem (see Hemming & Hawing, page 44).

Using your ruler, extend the tiny line that was the underarm seam of your cap sleeve. The length of this line should now be:

Underarm seam length + distance from Step 1 + hemming allowance

This line should follow the same angle of the side of your original cap sleeve *unless* this sleeve was too tight. If this is the case, you can increase the angle of your new line. Just make

SLEEVES PLEASE

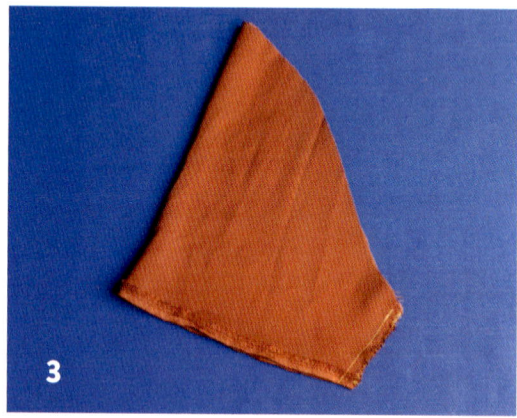

sure this new line is still angled in—if it becomes straight up and down or angled out, you'll be creating an entirely different sleeve style. That's not to say you can't do it, but I won't be teaching it, so you'll be fending for yourself.

Once you've extended your line on each side, use your ruler to draw a line connecting the bottoms of each of these lines. Your cap sleeve's hem likely curved upward, but since we're making an anti–cap sleeve, your hem should either be straight or curved slightly downward. You could get out a compass to make a perfect curve, but I got rid of mine after fifth grade math, so I just eyeball my curves.

Now cut out your new sleeves! Once you've cut them out, locate the three places you snipped the original sleeve's seam allowance. Make small cuts on your new sleeves in those exact same places.

Step 3: Prepare Your Sleeves

Let's get sewing! For this section, make sure you're repeating every step on the second sleeve.

Take one of your new sleeves and fold it in half with the right sides touching. Line up the two underarm seams and pin them together. Using a short–medium straight stitch, sew this seam using the seam allowance measurement from Step 2. Finish this seam allowance in the method of your choice (see Finishing Seams, page 32).

Now you're ready to hem your sleeve (see Hemming & Hawing, page 44). I always tend to leave this step until the end because I find hemming boring, but this is one of those great moments to learn from my shortcomings. It's so much easier to hem a sleeve when it's not attached to the rest of your garment, so heed my warning and hem it now.

The scrap fabric I used for my new sleeve was already hemmed, so technically I "hemmed" the sleeve before finishing the side seams. What can I say? I'm a rebel.

Step 4: Pin and Sew Your New Sleeves to Your Garment

Let's attach this new proper-length sleeve to your garment and finally let your scorned soul rest.

Your garment should be inside out, and your sleeves should be right side out. Put your sleeve into the armhole so the right sides of your sleeve and garment are touching. It should look like your jacket when you're trying to throw it on in a hurry but you can't put your arm through because the sleeve's facing the wrong way.

Match up the side seam of your garment with the underarm seam of your sleeve and pin them together. Next, match up and pin together the three cuts on your sleeve with the three cuts on your garment's seam allowance. With your anchor points in place, continue pinning your sleeve around the perimeter of the armhole. Then switch over to your sewing machine.

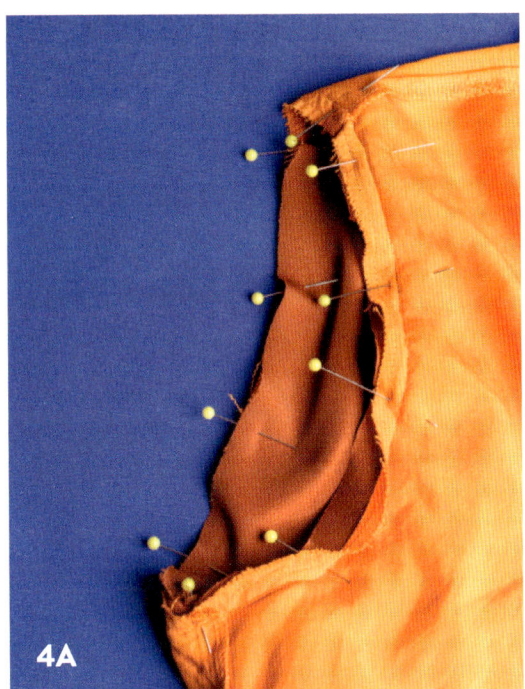

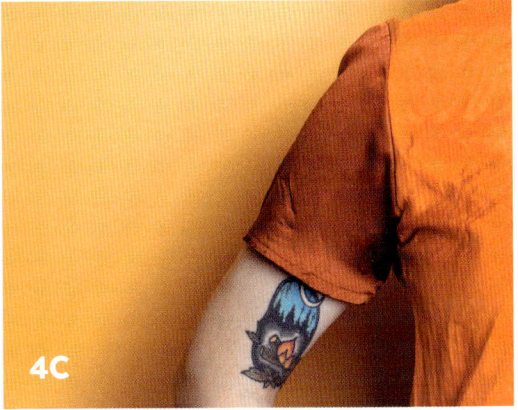

Oh hey!

If you've never attached a sleeve before, you may be very confused as to why the armhole is concave while the sleeve curve is convex. This confusion is very normal, but I promise these pieces fit together even if it doesn't look like they do. Just go one inch (2.5 cm) at a time matching up and pinning the edges of the sleeve and armhole, and you'll be amazed to see that they perfectly match up in the end.

You'll likely need to remove the front piece of your sewing machine so you can slide your whole sleeve around the machine. Using a short-medium straight stitch, sew around the perimeter of the sleeve. On the shoulder opening of your garment, you should be able to see where the original sleeve was attached. Follow this line with your stitching to replicate the original seam allowance. Finally, finish your seam allowance using either an overlocker or zigzag stitch.

As always, best practice is to give your new seam a final press with your iron. When ironing, your seam allowance should be facing in toward the center of your shirt. This will help your sleeve lie properly.

Do you feel that? That's the feeling of the top of your arm no longer being pinched. It feels good, doesn't it?

Ruffling Feathers ...and Sleeves

I'll never forget the time I went to the four-story Forever 21® in Times Square with my mom. I was in college on Staten Island and in need of some new clothes. I was 19 years old, peak Forever 21 demographic. Just one problem—I was also a U.S. size 14. My mom and I hunted the racks for anything in my size—across *four floors*—and came up with nothing. Finally on the bottom floor we discovered a literal corner of the store with a hanging neon sign: Plus Size. Four stories and a single corner for plus size.

Technically speaking, clothes exist for every size. But the pickings can be extremely slim depending on your size. Sure, there are clothes that fit you, but do they do anything to convey your personality or style? Or are they all just variations on a single style that the clothing manufacturer decided to grade to your size?

If you're sick of boring clothes, adding ruffles could be just the cure. They're the perfect way to add a design element to a dull shirt or lengthen a pair of shorts that are causing chub rub. We'll focus on adding ruffles to your sleeves in this tutorial, but it's easy to adapt this method to literally anything in need of the ol' razzle dazzle.

LEVEL

Intermediate

SUGGESTED FABRIC

Your ruffle fabric will need to be several inches wide and a lot longer than you first expect; you'll get these measurements in Step 2. As always, the extra fabric should be a similar type to your garment. The sturdier the fabric, the more structured a ruffle you can create! You'll need two spools of thread for this project—one that matches your garment and one that contrasts with it completely.

MATERIALS

Top in need of more exciting sleeves

Ruffle fabric

Ruler or measuring tape

Chalk or washable marker

Scissors

Pins

Iron

Seam ripper

Thread (two different colors)

Sewing machine

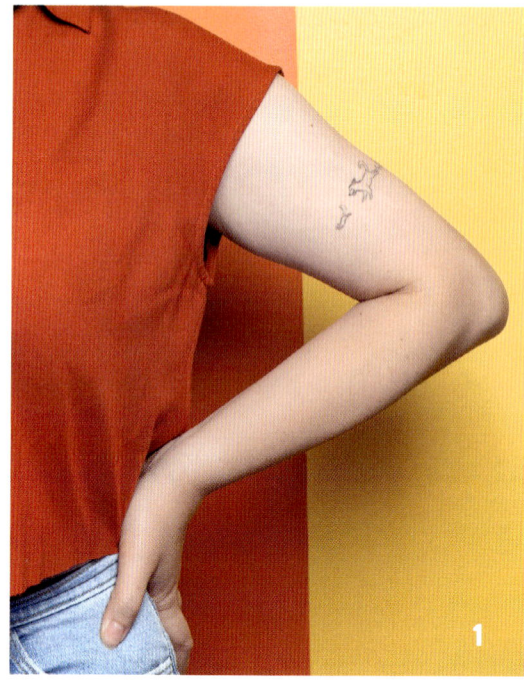

Step 1: Pick Your Shirt and Fabric

Which of your shirts or dresses is makeover ready? This could be a sleeveless top or one with existing sleeves that need a bit of length or flair (or both) at the bottom.

When selecting your fabric for your ruffles, as always, you'll want something that is a similar type to your garment. As for the color or pattern, it's entirely up to you! You decide if you want the ruffle to be the feature presentation or a supporting character. The main thing to look for in your fabric is length. Ruffles take a lot more fabric than you expect, just like sewing always takes much longer than you bargain for.

My preferred method for fabric matching is to grab a top that's at least a foot longer than you'd like. Then chop off the bottom, following Let's Crop About It (page 73), and repurpose that fabric for matching ruffles. That's what I did for this example!

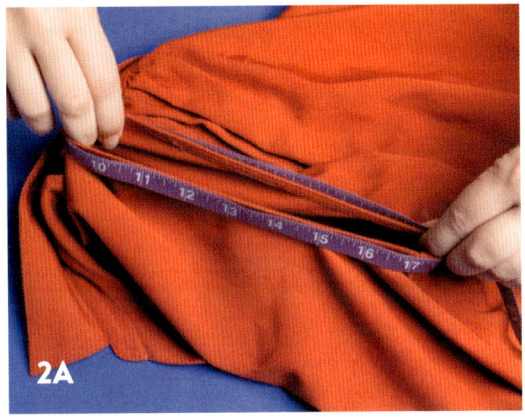

2A

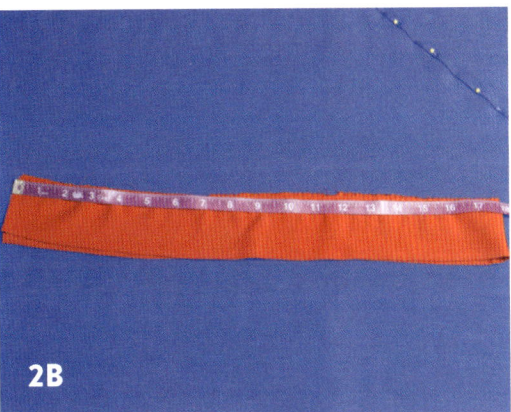

2B

The other important thing to consider is the wrong side of your ruffle fabric. Ruffles create lots of peaks and valleys, meaning there's a strong possibility the wrong side of your fabric will be visible in some places, especially if you're adding this to a sleeveless top. Lots of fabrics that have a design screen-printed on the right side are just plain white on the wrong side. If the white is going to totally clash with your garment, best to give the fabric a pass for this project.

Step 2: Determine Your Ruffle Size

Now let's play mathematician and collect some measurements so we can cut out two fabric rectangles to turn into ruffles.

With your garment laid down, measure the circumference of your sleeve opening. You can use a tape measure to measure all the way around the sleeve's hem by lining up the end of the tape with the underarm seam allowance and measuring around until you're back at the seam. Alternatively, lay your sleeve flat with one side on top of the other and use a ruler to measure from one side of the sleeve to the other, then multiply this measurement by two. The width of your final ruffle needs to be twice as long as your sleeve circumference to allow for maximum gathering, so we'll multiply the total circumference by two. Finally, add 1 inch (2.5 cm) to this measurement to account for a ½ inch (1.3 cm) seam allowance on each end. This will be the length of the rectangle of fabric we're about to cut.

(Circumference of sleeve opening x 2) + 1 inch (2.5 cm)

Next, decide how long you'd like the ruffle to be. You may want to put your garment on, look in the mirror, and visualize your ideal length. Personally, I like a 2-inch (5-cm) ruffle added to the bottom of a sleeve and a 3-inch (8-cm) ruffle added to a sleeveless top. But you've spent enough of your life letting clothing manufactures dictate what you wear, so don't take my word for it—make the ruffle length whatever your heart truly desires. In your final measurement for the length of your ruffle, you need to account for seam allowance and a hem, both of which we'll need an extra ½ inch (1.3 cm) for. If you're doing the math, you'll realize we'll be making a narrow hem for this ruffle. The width of your fabric rectangle should be:

Desired length of ruffle + 1 inch (2.5 cm)

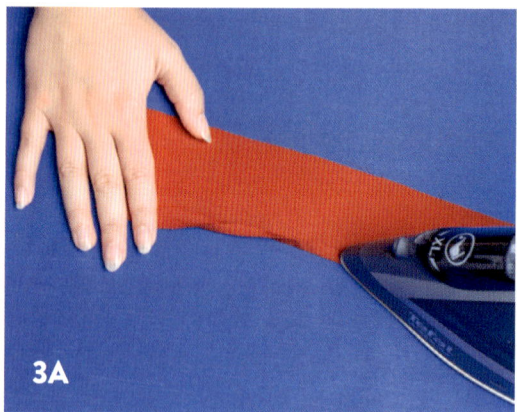

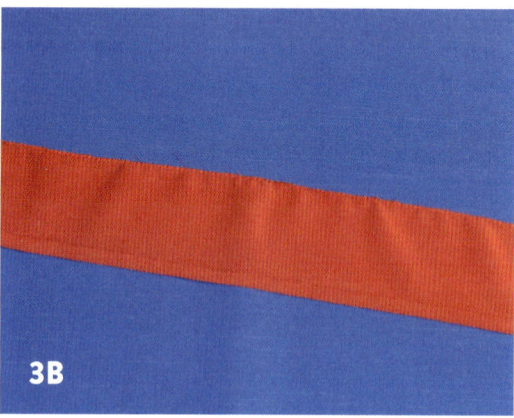

Your fact-finding mission is complete—you're ready to cut out your fabric rectangles. Fold your ruffle fabric in half lengthwise and draw a rectangle that is the length and width we just calculated. Pin your folded fabric in several places so it all stays in place while you cut it out. Speaking of which, cut it out! Your fabric rectangles, that is.

Step 3: Iron the Rectangles' Hems

Before we do anything else, we're going to partially create the hem on the bottom long edge of the rectangle. By that I mean we're going to iron the hem in place, but we won't pin or stitch it yet. While you may think you can skip this step, I promise it will be so much more annoying to do this later.

With the rectangle lying flat and the wrong side up, take one of the long edges and fold over ¼ inch (6.5 mm) of fabric and iron it in place (see Let's Get One Thing Straight, page 40). Now for some déjà vu: fold this ironed edge over another ¼ inch (6.5 mm) and iron it in place.

That's it for now—no sewing the hem in place yet. So why did we do this? Eventually, you are going to have to hem this ruffle, and it's a lot more difficult to iron a hem once one side of the rectangle is gathered. The hem isn't going to stay exactly in place without sewing it, but the pre-ironed folds will make a world of difference when it does come time to sew.

Now let's decide if we're going to finish the other long edge of your rectangle now or later (no, not finishing it at all is not an option). Because you'll be attaching this ruffle to your already hemmed garment, you need to decide whether you want to leave your sleeve's current hem intact or seam rip it open so it lays flatter and doesn't create a bulky seam. I always just leave the original hem intact because I'm a lazy sewist, but you don't need to follow my example! If you want to seam rip the original hem of your garment, go ahead and do that now (Let 'Er Rip: Seam Ripping, page 35), and then finish the seam in Step 7. If you're like me and want to keep the garment's hem intact, finish out this step.

Using a zigzag or overlocking stitch, finish the long edge of the rectangle that we didn't just "hem" (Finishing Seams, page 32).

Step 4: Baste the Rectangles

Time to start creating the gathers! There are a few different methods to create gathers, but I'm going to teach you the one I find to be the easiest and most reliable. If your definition of basting revolves around a Thanksgiving turkey, you may be confused when I tell you we're going to baste this rectangle. In sewing, basting is when we sew with our longest stitch with the intention of removing this stitching later. Basting is typically used to loosely hold together two pieces of fabric before finalizing the stitching in a later step (so technically we could have basted the hem in Step 3, but I'm trying to keep the annoying steps to a minimum, and it's really not going to make much of a difference).

We're going to use basting a bit differently for this tutorial. Select a thread that is a completely different color than your garment, then set your machine to a straight stitch with the longest possible stitch length. We're going to seam rip this thread out later, so don't worry about anyone witnessing the clash!

Lay your rectangle on your sewing machine with the unhemmed long edge lined up with the right side of your presser foot. It doesn't matter if the wrong or right side is facing up. Start sewing as close as you can to the short edge of the rectangle without getting the fabric stuck in your sewing machine. *Do not backstitch.* We're going to be pulling on these threads to create the gathers, so the beginning and end need to remain as untethered as a 20-something man whose ex-girlfriends are all "crazy."

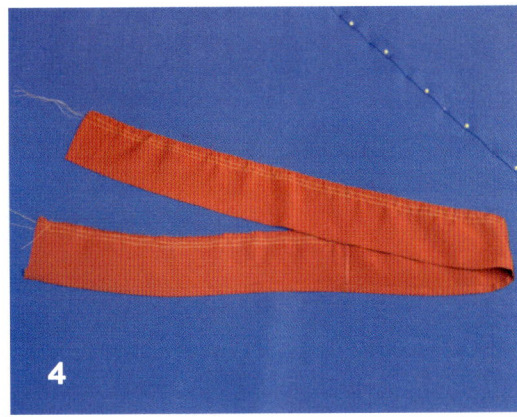

4

Sew a straight line all the way to the other end of the rectangle. When you get to the other end, pull your fabric away from your sewing machine until you have at least 3 inches (8 cm) of top and bobbin thread tailing behind your rectangle, then snip the thread.

Now for round two déjà vu—Déjà Vu: Electric Boogaloo. We're going to sew an identical line of stitching immediately to the left of the first line. Line up your first row of stitching with the right side of the presser foot and replicate the entire stitching and thread-tail process.

Step 5: Gather the Rectangles

Now enough with the prep work, it's time to get our hands dirty! (That's a figure of speech. If you have dirty hands, please wash them before touching your fabric.)

Just like any stitch, your basting stitches are made up of stitching from your top thread and your bobbin thread. We need to ensure that the tails of the top threads are on top of the fabric and the tails of the bobbin threads are underneath the fabric. If your top and bobbin threads are on the same side of your fabric, grab your seam ripper and ever so gently use it to pull up on the last stitch of the row to pull one of the tails to the other side of the fabric.

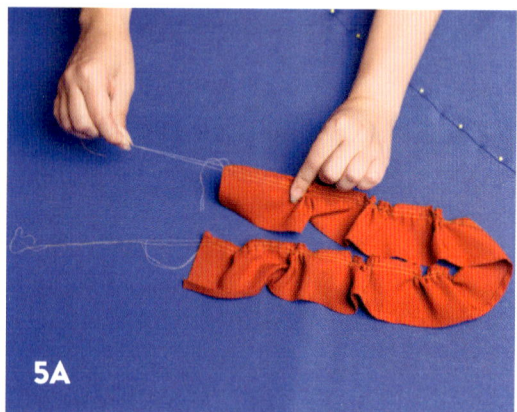

5A

5B

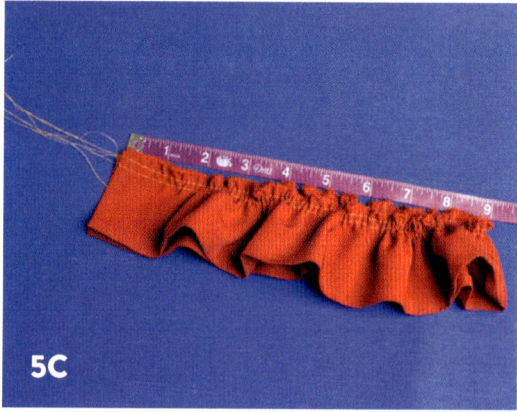

5C

Finally, let's gather! On one end of your rectangle, take the two top thread tails and tie them together in a knot. On the other end of the rectangle take the two bobbin thread tails and tie them together in a knot.

This may be difficult for all you Speed Racers because this step should be taken slowly. With one hand, hold on to one set of tied threads. Get your other hand prepped for the assist by pinching the fabric next to the tied threads with your thumb and index finger. Gently pull the tied threads while using your other hand to shimmy the fabric away from the tied threads.

Sorry to sound like your mom, but you need to be gentle during this process so as not to pull too hard and break the thread. However, if one of your threads breaks, that's OK! You can actually gather your fabric with a single line of basting, but the second line acts as insurance if one thread breaks.

Once you've managed to gather about half of the length of your fabric rectangle, you can start gathering from the other end. You can do all the gathering from just one side, but I find it easier to gather from both and meet in the middle. Your gathering is complete when the gathered edge is 1 inch (2.5 cm) longer than the length of your sleeve's circumference. It's OK if your gathers aren't evenly spaced at this point—we'll adjust them in the next step.

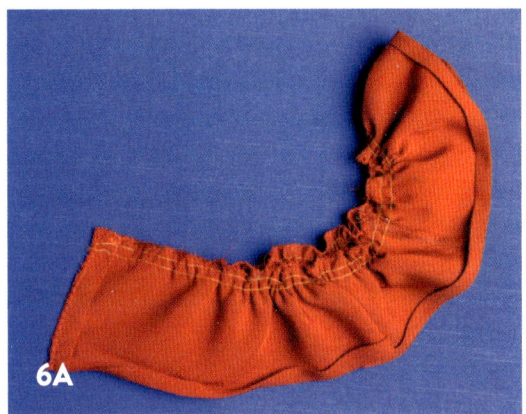
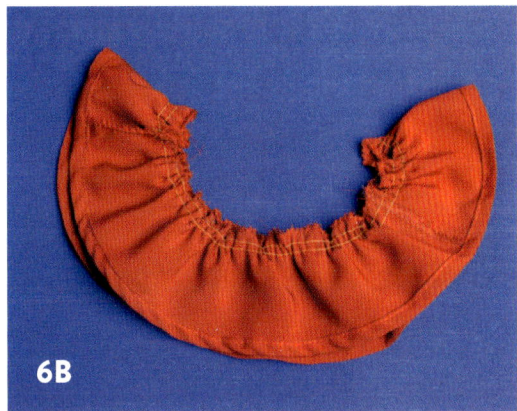

Step 6: Finish Your Ruffle Prep

Pin the short edges of the gathered rectangle together with the right sides touching. Switch out the thread in your machine to one that matches your garment. Using a short–medium straight stitch, sew the sides together with a ½-inch (1.3-cm) seam allowance, backstitching at the beginning and end. Make sure the thread tails from your gathering are extended over the seam allowance as you sew so as not to tangle them in your stitching. Once the seam is stitched together, you can trim your thread tails short. Finish this seam with a zigzag or overlocking stitch.

Then we're ready to even out the gathers. There's not an exact science to spacing your gathers, and if there is, I don't want to know. We're just going to eyeball this. Slide your ruffles along your threads to evenly spread them out along the circumference of the ruffle.

Now it's time to choose your own adventure. Maybe not as exciting as choosing which monster you'll follow in a *Goosebumps* book, but you at least get to choose if you're going to hem your rectangle or attach your gathers to your sleeve first. A pro for hemming first is that it's always easier to hem a sleeve when it doesn't have a garment attached to the other end. A pro for attaching the gathers first is that you don't risk the gathers getting loose or wonky while you sew the hem.

To finish the hem, refold the fabric following the creases we ironed earlier, pin them in place, and edgestitch the hem in place with a medium straight stitch. If you need a refresher, head back to Hemming & Hawing (page 44). Alternatively, visit Step 7 and sew your gathers in place before returning here for the hemming.

Step 7: Pin and Sew Your Ruffle to Your Garment

With your garment right side out, turn your ruffle inside out and line up the gathered edge of your ruffle with the edge of your sleeve opening. The right sides should be touching, and the body of your ruffle should be wrapped around your sleeve, not hanging below it. If your garment doesn't have sleeves, line up the side seam of the ruffle with the underarm or armpit seam. Pin the ruffle to the sleeve starting at the seams, then continue pinning all the way around the sleeve's perimeter.

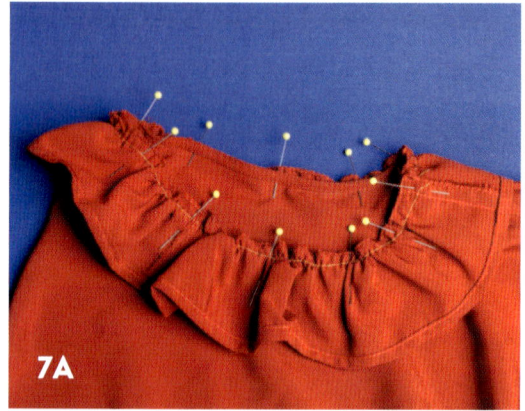

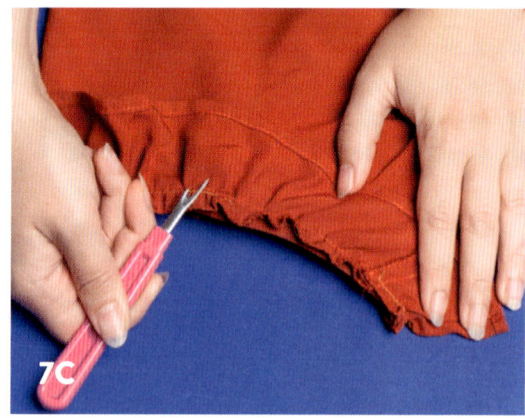

Once more to the sewing machine with feeling. Place your sleeve around your sewing machine with the ruffles facing up. Select a short–medium straight stitch and place your needle ½ inch (1.3 cm) in from the ruffle/garment edge.

Now we're ready to sew around the circumference of the sleeve and ruffle! Yet again, I recommend going slowly with this step. When I first started sewing ruffles, I'd find that my presser foot would push all the gathers forward as I sewed, leaving me with long stretches of no gathers and then suddenly *boom!*—all the gathers shoved into one section. To prevent this, use your fingers to hold the gathers in place as you gently push your fabric through your machine. Make sure to backstitch at the beginning and end and *avoid sewing over the thread you used to gather the ruffle*. It's not the end of the world if you stitch over these, but we'll be seam ripping these out imminently and it's so irritating to do when your other stitching overlaps.

Speak of the devil, it's time to seam rip out the gathering stitches. If you listened to my instructions at the beginning, you'll be so grateful you stitched with a contrasting color, making it easy to identify the stitching you should remove. If you didn't, well, then what did we learn?

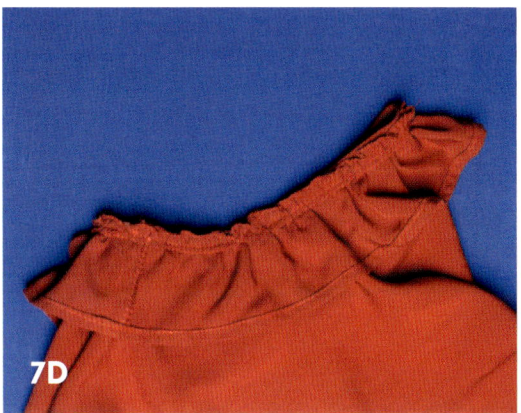

Finally, one last stitch and we're done! (Except for the fact that you probably now need to repeat all of this on the other side of your garment.) If you kept your garment's hem intact and finished the raw edge of your ruffle in Step 3, you need to add a second line of stitching along the seam allowance. On your sewing machine, place your needle about ¼ inch (6.5 mm) to the side of your seam so it's on the seam allowance. Use a medium straight stitch to sew again around the circumference of your seam allowance, backstitching at the beginning and end.

If you instead chose to seam rip your garment's hem in Step 3, sew your garment and ruffle seam allowance together with a zigzag or overlocking stitch (Finishing Seams, page 32).

Step 8: Iron Your Seams

I know, I know; you did so much prep work for this project and you're ready to be finished. Just one small piece of post-work and we're done! We just need to iron the seam allowance so your ruffle lies correctly.

Turn your garment inside out, place your sleeve around the end of your ironing board, and fold your seam allowance away from your ruffle. Iron your seam allowance to this side along the ruffle's circumference. Try to avoid pressing on the actual gathers too much, as ruffles are meant to be wild and free, not caged (or pressed in place).

You are also welcome to go one step further to keep your ruffle's seam flat. For this option, keep your seam allowance folded away from the ruffle and turn your garment right side out. Use a medium-long straight stitch to topstitch your seam allowance to your garment about ¼ inch (6.5 mm) up from the seam. That said, this has been a long tutorial, and your ruffle will be just fine if you don't do this final step.

At last, we are finished giving your garment some much-needed personality (as soon as you repeat all the steps on the other side). I challenge you to add ruffles to the hems of as many boring garments as you can and really ruffle the feathers of the fashion industry.

Pick a Pocket or Two

Sometimes I make really clever jokes about altering clothes. Other times, I'm just mad that the need to alter exists. Case in point: pockets. Why. Don't. Women. Have. Them. Luckily, I've spent years perfecting my pocket game, and I'm here to bestow that knowledge upon you.

The reality is that pockets are quite easy to add to clothing. I know it's unfair that we have to do it ourselves, but think of the benefits! Our pockets can be the exact shape and size we want—no more hoping our phones won't fall to the floor and smash. They can be any color or pattern we desire, perfectly conveying our personality to the world. They can sit *exactly* where we need them—no more awkwardly bending our arms for pockets that are too high on our jackets.

By the end of this chapter, you'll have so many pockets you won't have a *clue* which one you left your phone, keys, wallet, sunglasses, spare pen, doggy bags, receipts, lip gloss, or seam ripper in. I don't know about you, but I'm going to lose all these things with or without pockets, so I'd rather have enough pockets to take on the patriarchy while I do it.

The Outsider: External Pockets

In my opinion, external pockets are the easiest pocket type to add to your clothing. There's no seam ripping, facing, or cutting of your garment required—almost all of the work takes place before even touching your garment. You can add external pockets well and truly *anywhere* you want—pants, skirts, dresses, shirts, sleeves. You can even sew one to your pet's clothes if you are truly passionate about pocket equality.

LEVEL
Confident Beginner

SUGGESTED FABRIC
100 percent of this pocket will be visible, so fabric choice is important. Do you want it to stand out with highly contrasting colors as a blazing emblem of the injustice that none of your clothes came with pockets? Or do you want to fly under the radar, quietly plotting your overthrow of the patriarchy with fabric that blends in with the rest of the garment? The fabric should be woven, sturdy, and thick. Its entire purpose is to hold all our necessities in place, so thin, stretchy fabrics won't cut it here.

MATERIALS
Pocketless clothing

Pocket fabric

Ruler or measuring tape

Chalk or washable marker

Scissors

Iron

Thread

Sewing machine

Chopstick or similar-shaped object

Pins

 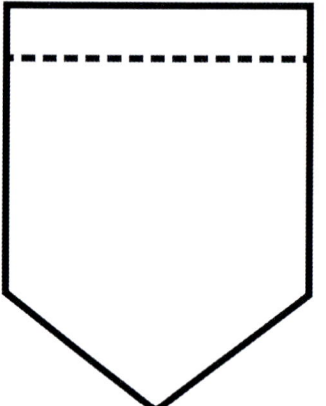 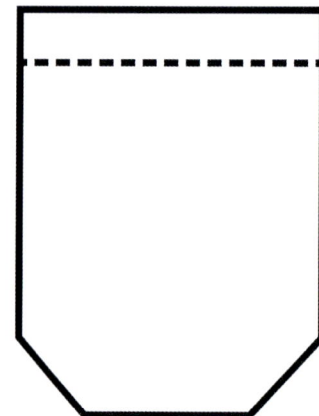

Pocket (shape) options!

Step 1: Pick, Measure, and Cut Your Pocket

Let's pick our pocket type and size! The mainstay shapes of the external pocket game are rectangles, pentagons, and hexagons, but don't limit yourself if you've been dreaming of a decagonal pocket. That said, I personally recommend choosing from the above options when you're just starting out.

The two most important measurements to take when making a pocket are the width of your hand and the height of your phone. I mean, come on, retailers—don't act like you've done women a massive service by giving us a pocket barely deep enough to cover our phone's camera.

I like to make the opening of my pockets 1 inch (2.5 cm) wider than the widest part of my hand (usually the distance between your bottom knuckles on your pinkie and thumb) and 1 to 2 inches (2.5 to 5 cm) taller than my phone. I've learned the hard way that making

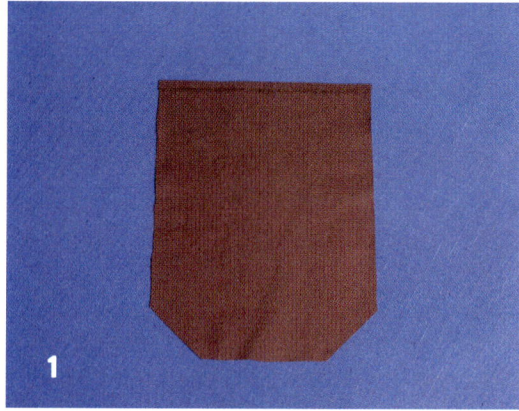

a pocket as deep as possible to make up for decades of going without doesn't actually solve anything; it just means you have to awkwardly dig for your phone around your knees.

Once you've picked your shape, height, and width, cut out however many pockets your heart desires. Include a 1-inch (2.5-cm) seam allowance on the opening and ⅝-inch (1.6-cm) seam allowance on all other sides. If you own pinking shears (or alarmingly sharp kids' crazy scissors) I recommend using them since you typically don't finish every raw edge of pockets.

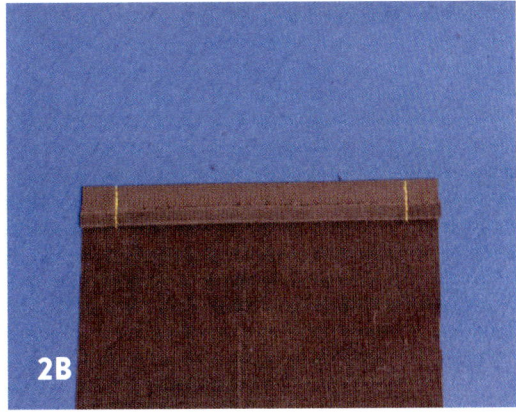

Oh hey!

Pinking shears are scissors that cut a zigzag pattern. Woven fabrics are made of vertical and horizontal threads, so cutting straight on the grain line means that all the threads parallel to the cut can just slip off. This is what fraying is. When you use pinking shears to make angled cuts, the woven threads can't slip off as easily.

Step 2: Create the Pocket Opening

Off to the iron! If you have a wrong side of the fabric, place that face up and give it its only moment to shine. Grab the edge of the fabric at the top of your pocket, fold it over ¼ inch (6.5 mm), and iron it in place (see Let's Get One Thing Straight, page 40). This baby fold is responsible for hiding the top raw edge in our final pocket. If I were writing a self-help book, this would be the small-change-big-impact section.

Now flip the fabric over so the right side is facing up. With the baby fold still folded under on the opposite side, fold the new top edge of the pocket down ¾ inch (1.9 cm) and iron it in place. Your baby fold will now be at the very bottom of this new fold.

Now we need to secure these folds in place, which is the same thing I say when I put on rigid jeans over my stomach rolls. On your sewing machine, line up your needle with the top of the pocket, ⅝ inch (1.6 cm) in from the side. Using a medium straight stitch, sew a straight line down from the top of the pocket to the bottom of the fold. Repeat this on the other side. It's OK if you sew a couple stitches beyond the bottom of the fold—this can actually be helpful for what's to come.

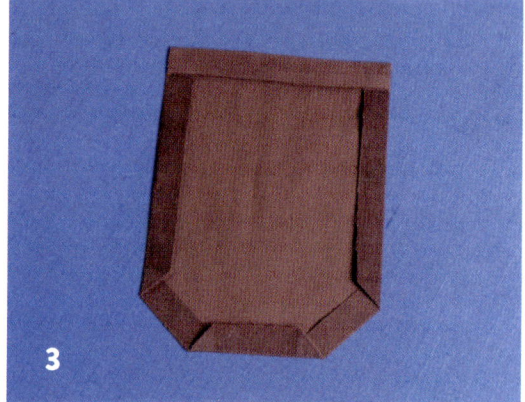

Time to turn these right side out! To make the top corners of our pocket nice and sharp, we need to clip the corners at the very top of our seam allowance. At the top of the pocket, make an angled cut that begins 1 to 2 millimeters to the outside of the stitches and extends to the fabric's outer edge. The cut should end roughly at the bottom of the folds. Avoid snipping any of the stitches or you will be left with some tiny holes in the top corners of your pockets. We clip the corners of the seam allowance so that our pocket corners will be flat and sharp when they're turned right-side out, instead of bulky.

Now fold the top of the pocket right-side out. You'll see the side seam allowance naturally starts to turn under as well (this is where having those extra stitches below the fold can help as a little folding guide).

Now the top of our pocket should look almost complete, but it probably has some inward-turned corners. We want the corners to be as sharp as a good cheddar, so we need to use a small object to poke out the corners. I typically use a narrow chopstick or the tip of an unclicked ballpoint pen. Something too thin and sharp like a seam ripper will poke a hole in your corner.

With that, you officially have the top of your pocket—congrats, babe!

Step 3: Fold and Iron the Pocket Sides

Now we need to get the other sides of the pocket ready. Luckily, this is much simpler than prepping the opening.

With the wrong side of the pocket facing up, fold all remaining sides in ⅝ inch (1.6 cm) and iron them in place. Unlike the opening, we only need to fold the edges in once—no extra baby folds. I don't know who decided it's standard practice to keep the inside pocket edges raw, but my lazy bones thank them.

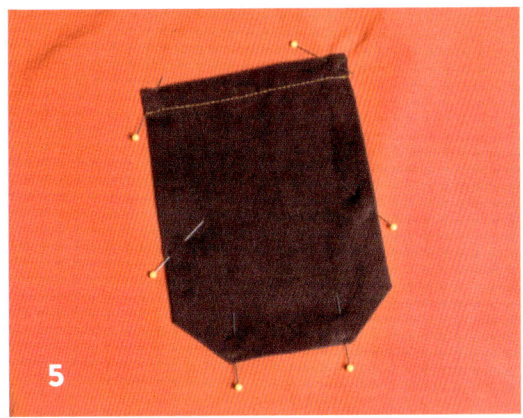

Step 4: Topstitch the Top of Your Pocket

One last step before we're ready to attach the pocket to our clothes! We need to completely secure the top folds of the pocket opening. Topstitch across the opening fold, sewing as close as you can to the bottom edge of the fold.

Place your pocket on your machine wrong side up and line up your needle with the bottom fold of your pocket opening. Select a medium-long stitch length and edgestitch along the entire fold, backstitching at the beginning and end. It's imperative you do this before attaching the pocket to your garment. If you try to do this when the pocket is on your garment, you'll end up sewing the pocket shut and participating in fake pockets, and is that really the side of history you want to be on?

This is also the time that you can add any decorative stitching to your pocket if you're fancy or have been dying to test the embroidery stitches on your sewing machine.

Step 5: Pin Your Pocket to Your Garment

Now we're ready to attach the pocket to your garment and give your hand the home it deserves! Even if you think you know exactly where you want the pocket, make sure to pin it on your garment, try it on, and have a look in the mirror. A pocket can look straight when it's laying on a flat garment and then surprise you by looking completely askew once your body's curves get involved. I have absolutely sewn pockets on super securely, looked in the mirror *after*, and discovered that I was going to need to seam rip them off, adjust the angle, and resew. Don't be an Allie (do be an ally though).

Once you've got the angle right (or obtuse [Sorry, geometry joke]), finish pinning all sides of your pocket to your garment.

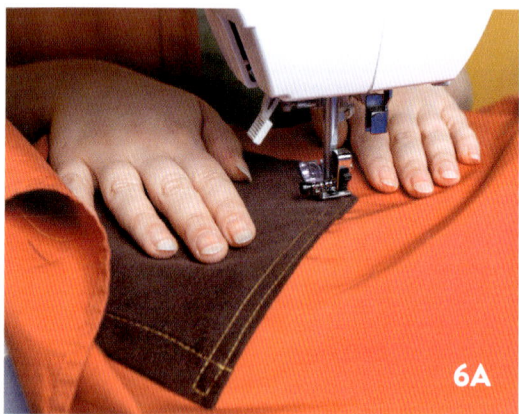

Oh hey!

If you're attaching this pocket to a stretchy garment, put on the garment, place the pocket in your desired position and mark where each corner is with a bit of chalk. Once you take the garment off, lay the pocket down on it and see if the marks are narrower than the pocket. If they are, that's fine! Pin your pocket corners to the marks. When you're sewing, you'll need to stretch your garment as you go so that the pocket lays flat on the garment. If you just sew the pocket flat without stretching, you run the very real risk of preventing your clothing from stretching and making it uncomfortably tight in some places. Let's not fix one problem just to make another!

Step 6: Sew the Pocket to Your Garment

We're going to topstitch all the edges (except the opening, obviously). On your sewing machine, select a medium straight stitch and line up your needle with one of the far sides of your pocket opening. I suggest you begin stitching ⅛ inch (3 mm) in from the side and top of your pocket.

When you reach the end of each edge with your machine, there's no need to completely stop and restart your sewing with a brand new line of stitching. When you get ⅛ inch (3 mm) from the end of the line, place your needle through your garment in the down position, lift your presser foot, turn your garment to line up the next edge with your needle, place your presser foot down, and keep on sewing!

You can stitch each edge just once, or double back and add a second line of stitching roughly ⅛ inch (3 mm) away to give your pocket a stronger hold. To do this, when you get all the way around the edges and back to the opening, turn your pocket 90 degrees in toward the center, stitch two or three stitches

across the top of the pocket, then turn it a further 90 degrees and start sewing along all the sides again. Finish by replicating those same two to three stitches on the other side of the pocket. As always, backstitch at the beginning and end.

If you opt for a single line of stitching, it's important to reinforce the stitching on the corners on either side of the opening. The openings of our pockets receive a lot of action from pushing our hands and other objects down, especially if, like me, you are always running late for your train and shoving your keys, phone, cards, lip gloss, mascara, earrings, and a necklace in them while flying out the door.

We're going to sew a triangle on each side of the pocket opening to both reinforce it and our relationship with the Illuminati. Shoot, I promised I would stop telling people that. Once you've sewn around the edges and get back to the opening, turn the pocket 90 degrees toward the center and sew three to four stitches in toward the opening, then continue turning the pocket another 45 degrees and sew until you hit the side stitches. Backstitch in place, and voilà—a triangle!

Sewing the triangle on the final corner is pretty easy because we get to use the perimeter stitch as a guide. Sewing the triangle on the first corner before stitching the perimeter? That's a bit trickier. The obvious solution is to mark out the triangles with some chalk so you can just sew along the lines. However, if you're a fly-by-the-seat-of-your-pants sewist like me, you can either just wing it or return to the first corner after sewing the perimeter and stitch in the triangle's last two sides. I won't tell anyone your secret.

Don't stress if your triangles aren't perfectly identical. Honestly, no one is paying close attention to your pockets (unless they're preparing to pickpocket you, in which case do you really value their opinion?). Whenever I sew these corners, they're always sisters, but never twins.

At last! We have a pocket! For some of you, this could be your first one ever. How do you feel? Ready for world domination? Good. We ride at dawn.

The Inside Job: Seam Pockets

Is there any greater feeling than trying on a dress that you look incredible in and assuming it couldn't get any better—until you place your hands on your hips and find they slide into pockets? Actually, finding affordable housing is a greater feeling, but let's take what we can get, yeah? This might make you mad knowing how many dresses don't come with pockets, but it's seriously not difficult to add side seam pockets.

My best foresight was adding seam pockets to my bridesmaid dress for my best friend's wedding. I found out at the rehearsal that I was responsible for holding onto her soon-to-be-husband's ring (no pressure), but luckily, I had the perfect secret compartment to hold it.

Adding a side seam pocket isn't exclusive to dresses. This same method will work for pants, skirts, or shorts. A word of caution: this isn't the ideal method for jeans as they typically have a more complex side seam. But also, jeans shouldn't come without pockets. If they do, they should be charged with a felony.

LEVEL
Intermediate

SUGGESTED FABRIC
As the title suggests, your pocketless garment needs to have a seam—specifically a side seam. Your pocket should be a sturdier woven fabric so that the pocket has the integrity to keep its shape and hold your stuff (which is a lot more integrity than the people who keep making women's clothes without pockets have). This fabric will be minimally visible, so it doesn't need to be the matchiest of fabric to your garment. It will mostly only be seen if you're carrying something really heavy that pulls your seam open a bit or if you turn your pockets out to illustrate that you have no money because you had to spend it all on handbags.

MATERIALS

Pocketless garment with a side seam

Chalk or washable marker

Pins

Ruler or measuring tape

Scissors

Seam ripper

Pocket fabric

Thread

Sewing machine

Iron

Step 1: Open Your Seam Where Your Pocket Will Be

Try on your pocketless garment. Place your hands along the side seams in the position that feels most comfortable when saying "Thanks, it has pockets!" With chalk, markers, or pins, mark on the seam where the top and bottom of your hand would enter this pocket. For this purpose, the bottom of your hand is your lowest pinkie knuckle, and the top of your hand is your lowest thumb knuckle.

Take your garment off. Mark 1 inch (2.5 cm) above your top mark and 1 inch (2.5 cm) below your bottom mark. This extra space is going to account for our pocket's seam allowance and any additional space you need to pull your hand out when it's balled in a fist around whatever you're storing in your pocket. Measure the distance between your two new marks and write it down if you want to remember it (or don't write it down if you want to be scrambling for your tape measure again later like me).

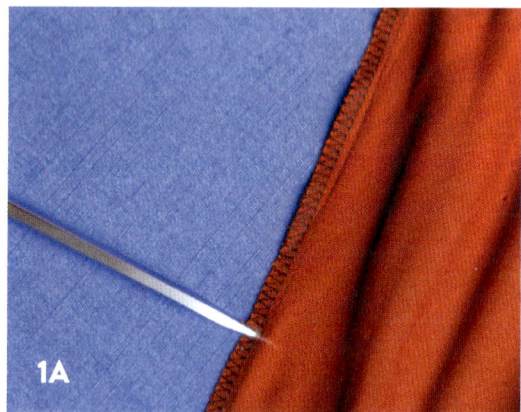

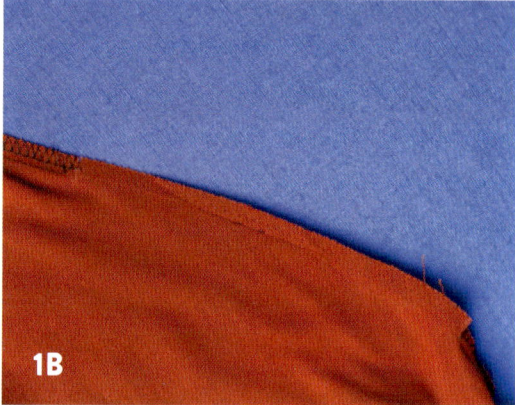

Before you seam rip open the seam, use scissors to snip the seam allowance in the same places you've marked the ends of your pocket. The easiest way to line this up is to stick a pin straight through your mark on your right side, then line up your cut with that pin on the wrong side. Don't cut all the way through the seam allowance to the seam. This cut is just a small mark that we'll use as a guide to line up our pocket patterns later.

Now seam rip open the side seam between the two marks.

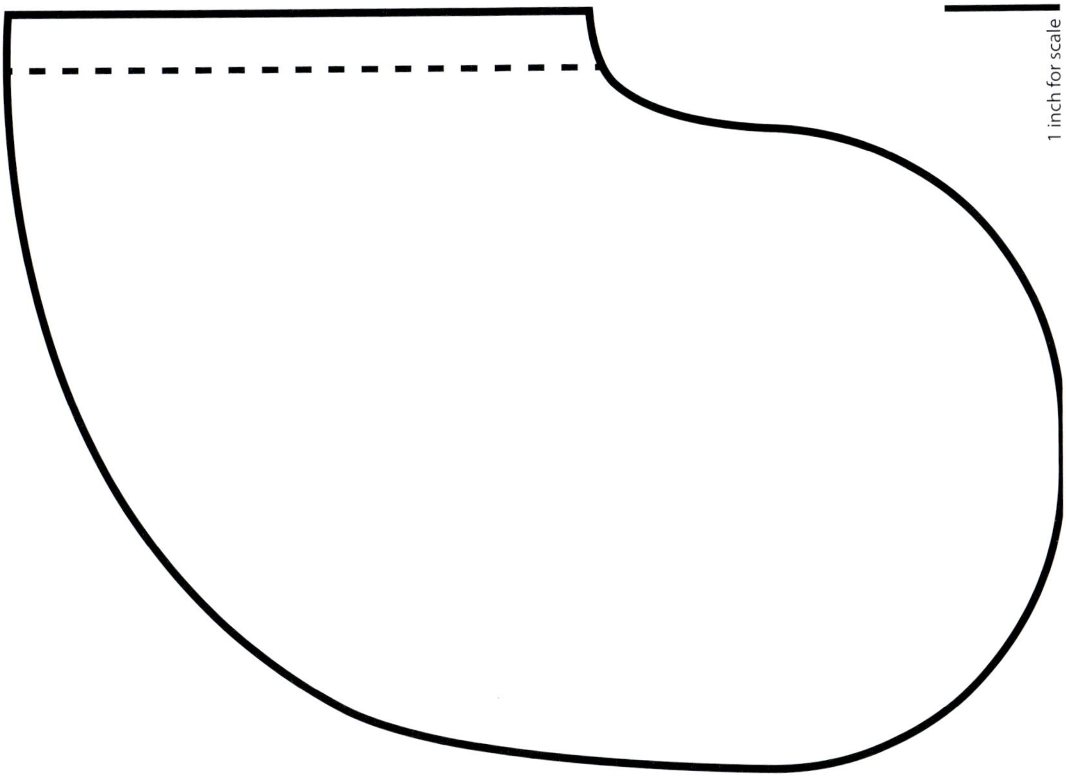

1 inch for scale

Step 2: Cut Out Your Pocket Fabric

Let's start making the pocket bag! A pocket bag looks like an ankle sock turned 90 degrees. The ankle bit of the sock is the bit that we'll attach to the side seams of the garment. The foot bit of the sock is where you'll store all your stuff. (I'm suddenly inspired to turn all my socks into pockets.)

I've made a template for you based on the size of my hand and the height and width of my phone. If your hand is the exact same size as mine, aren't you lucky? If it's not, just adjust your pattern for your measurements. Remember when I told you to write down the width of your hand? Well, add 2 inches (5 cm) to that, and that's how long the vertical line on your pocket pattern needs to be:

Widest part of your hand + 2 inches (5 cm)

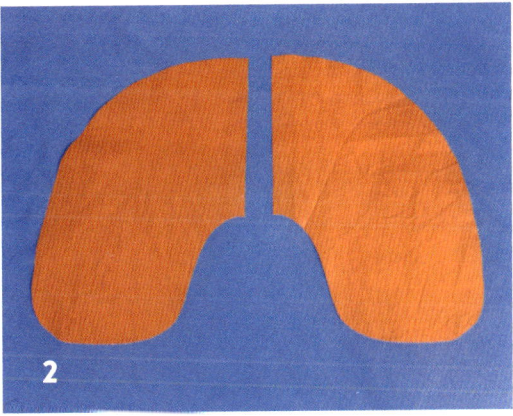

Yes, they do look like lungs.

The length and width of the pocket should be the size of your phone, remembering to account for the ½-inch (1.3-cm) seam allowance that will run the perimeter of your pocket bag. I've included this in my pattern.

Cut out two pieces of your pocket pattern for every pocket you're adding.

PICK A POCKET OR TWO

Step 3: Attach Your Pocket to the Garment's Seam

We're going to add each side of the pocket bag one at a time to the garment. With the front of your garment right side out, place one side of your pocket bag right side down. Match up the straight line of your pocket bag with your garment's side seam, lining up the ends of the straight line edges of the pocket bag with the seam allowance snips from Step 1.

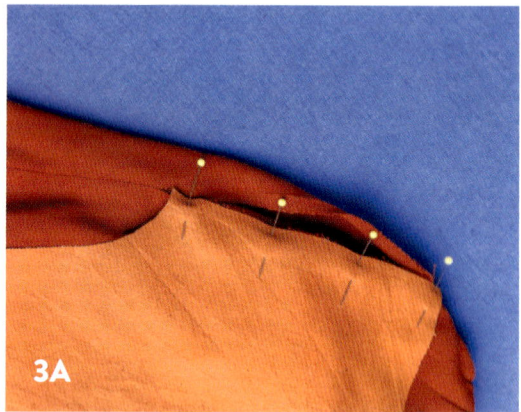

If at any point you find your working space is too tight, you can seam rip your garment's seam open a bit further; we'll just sew it closed later.

Using a short–medium straight stitch, stitch the pocket to the seam allowance. Your stitch should follow exactly where the seam was originally stitched together.

Repeat this process on the back half of the garment. On the back half of the pocket bag only, sew another line of straight stitching along the seam allowance ¼ inch (6.5 mm) away from your seam. We're not going to zigzag stitch or overlock this edge, so this second line of stitching is our insurance in case your pocket starts to rip from all the heavy objects you'll probably start carrying around now just because you can.

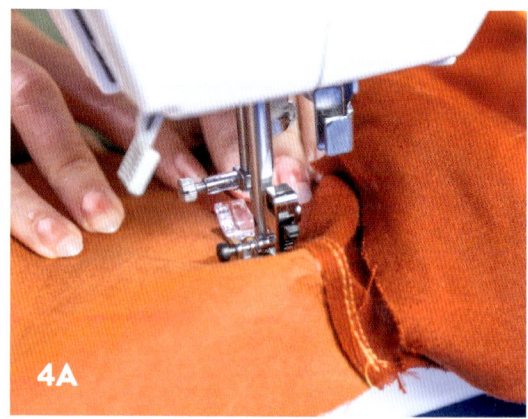

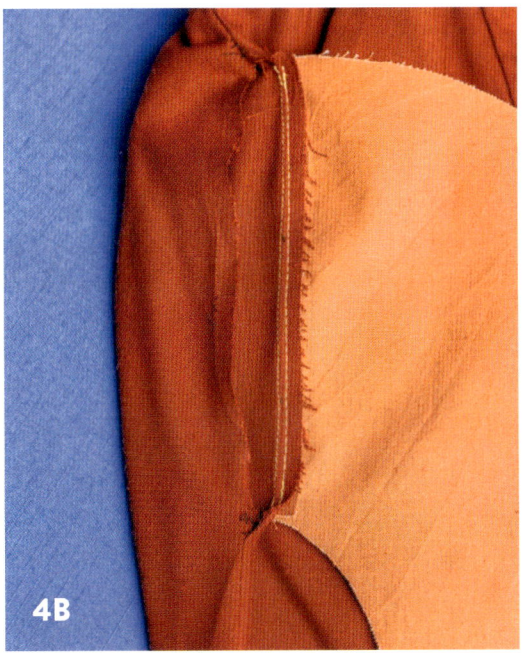
Understitching on the wrong side of the pocket bag.

Understitching on the right side of the pocket bag.

Step 4: Understitch the Front Piece of Your Pocket Bag

Now we're going to understitch **only the front piece** of the pocket bag. Understitching is used to keep facing or pocket fabric from revealing itself to the outside world. It is a second straight stitch near a seam that prevents the inside fabric from rolling outward. Essentially, understitching is a secret-keeper.

To understitch, take the seam allowance of both the front pocket bag and the garment and fold both toward the wrong side of the pocket bag. Using a medium–long straight stitch, stitch both seam allowances to just the pocket bag around ⅛ inch (3 mm) from the seam. I like to gently pull the two pieces on either side of the seam apart as I understitch. This further encourages the pocket fabric to stay hidden (can't let the patriarchy know we have pockets now or they'll try to take them away).

Oh hey!

Understitching can be used on many garments and other sewing projects—like necklines with facing or jackets and shirts with plackets. The trickiest thing is just remembering which side of the fabric to fold and stitch the seam allowance to. The trick is to always fold and stitch onto the fabric that should not be seen. We want the stitching and the inner fabric hidden from view.

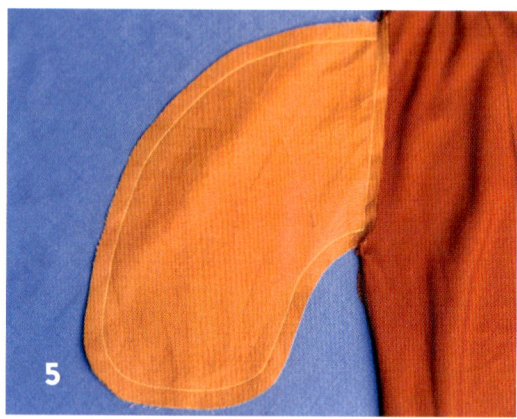

Step 5: Sew the Pocket Together

Now to sew everything together so this pocket can reach its full potential. Put both sides of the pocket bag inside your garment, then turn the whole garment inside out. Pin both sides of the pocket bag together with the right sides touching. We're going to stitch these together using a short–medium straight stitch and a ½-inch (1.3-cm) seam allowance. Line up your needle with the seam where the pocket bag is sewn to your garment. Continue sewing around the entire perimeter of the bag until you reach the garment's side seam on the other side. Backstitch at the beginning and end.

Step 6: Finish the Seams

Let's play doctor and stitch back up the garment seam we previously cut open. With your garment inside out, place it on your sewing machine so the pocket bag is to the right of the needle and all the seam allowances are folded toward the pocket bag.

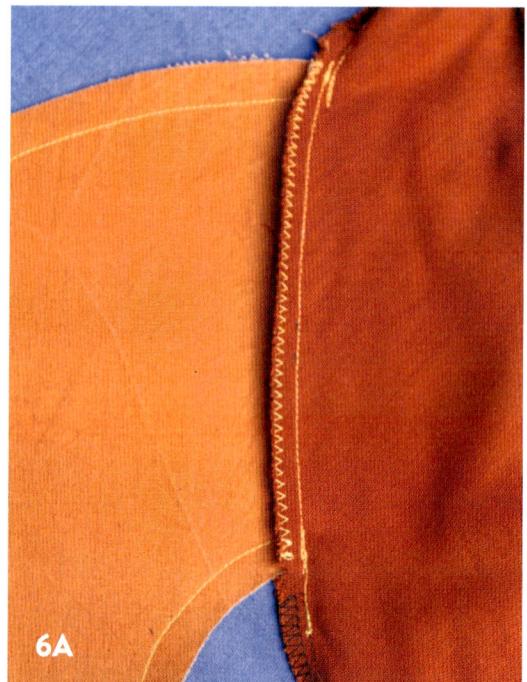

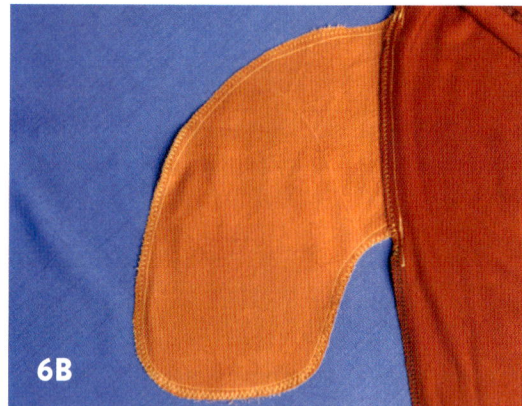

We'll start by stitching along the garment's original seam above the pocket. I like to start restitching the garment seam about ½ inch (1.3 cm) above where it's seam ripped. This helps resecure the current seam stitches that we weakened by ripping the rest of the seam. Using a short–medium straight stitch, backstitch, then retrace the garment's seam stitches exactly until you get to your pocket bag.

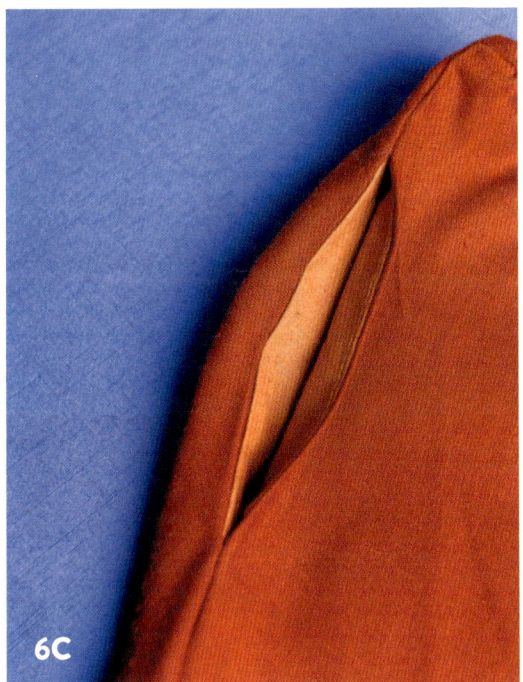

6C

Using a zigzag stitch or overlocker, sew along the last inch of the garment's seam allowance, then continue your stitch along the pocket bag seam allowance and onto an inch (2.5 cm) of garment seam allowance on the other side of the pocket. Backstitch at the beginning and end (see Finishing Seams, page 32).

Now all that's left is to turn your garment right side out, keeping the pocket where it belongs inside the garment, and iron the seam flat. That and repeating this entire process on the other side of your garment if you're adding a second pocket.

Put on that garment, slide your hands into those pockets, look to the skies, and proudly proclaim, "Thanks, it has pockets!"

When you reach the pocket bag, sew ever so slightly to the left of the original seam allowance while giving your pocket a slight tug to the right. This ensures that the pocket's seam allowance doesn't peek through to the outside of the garment. Finish your stitch with a backstitch one or two stitches beyond the pocket's ½-inch (1.3-cm) seam allowance. Repeat this process on the bottom of the pocket opening.

Now we just need to finish the seam allowance and you'll have the pocket of your dreams! Instead of sewing only the pocket seam allowance, I like to finish the seam allowance starting along the last inch (2.5 cm) of the garment's seam allowance. This helps us keep the garment seam allowance from unraveling now that it's been seam ripped, and it gives us one more way to secure the pocket to our garment.

Glossary: Words You'll Actually Use

Backstitch—A method to lock your stitching in place at the beginning and end of sewing. Sew forward two to three stitches, then sew backward two to three stitches, then continue sewing forward, all along the same line. You can learn all about this in Meet Your Sewing Machine (page 25).

Basting—Sewing with your longest stitch length with the intention of removing this stitching later. Basting is typically used to loosely hold together two pieces of fabric before finalizing the stitching in a later step. It is also used to assist in gathering fabric. You can give basting a try in Ruffling Feathers . . . and Sleeves (page 155).

Bobbin—A small spool of thread that sits inside your sewing machine below the needle. It catches the thread from the top of your machine and holds the stitches in place. For more on winding your own bobbins, check out page 14.

Clipping a Corner—Using scissors to cut a triangle of seam allowance off a corner of fabric. This is done before turning the fabric right side out to prevent any fabric from bulking up in the corner.

Dart—Folded fabric sewn together to create three-dimensional curves. Often used to make garments fit better around your bust and waist. I'll teach you all about darts in Get This Party Darted (page 48) and The Real World: Dart Edition (page 53).

Dart Legs—Two lines that meet in a point. These two lines are sewn together to create a fold that makes fabric three-dimensional (a dart).

Dart Point—Where two dart legs meet at a tip.

Edgestitching—Using a straight stitch to sew as close to the edge of a seam, hem, or fold as possible.

Facing—A separate piece of fabric used to finish a raw edge as an alternative to hemming. Facing is sewn along the raw edge of a garment with the right sides touching. It is then folded to the inside of the garment to conceal the raw edge. We'll utilize facing in Hips & Thighs Don't Lie (page 113).

Gathering—Bunching fabric together to create a ruffle or decorative neckline, sleeve, etc. We'll gather together to learn this in Ruffling Feathers . . . and Sleeves (page 155).

Interfacing—A special fabric attached to the wrong side of a fabric to make it stiffer/sturdier. It comes in fusible (iron-on) and nonfusible versions in light, medium, and heavy weights. To learn how to add interfacing, head on over to The (Fabric) Choice is Yours (page 20).

Overlocking Stitch—A stitch comprised of two to four separate threads used to finish a raw edge. Some of the threads will create a straight stitch and others will loop around the fabric's edge. This stitch is only available on an overlocker/serger, not a standard sewing machine.

Pinking Shears—Special scissors that cut a zigzag pattern. Pinking shears are used to help prevent woven fabrics from unraveling or fraying like they do when cut with straight scissors. To see what pinking shears look like, check out The Outsider: External Pockets (page 167).

Pocket Bag—The part of your pocket that lives just inside the pocket opening and holds all your stuff. It's the bit of fabric you pull out to show you don't have any money. We'll create and sew our own in The Inside Job: Seam Pockets (page 175).

Presser Foot—A small piece of metal attached to your sewing machine that holds the fabric flat and in place while you sew. The essential presser feet to have on hand are the standard, zipper, and walking foot. I introduce you to all of these feet in Meet Your Sewing Machine (page 25).

Quilting or Patchwork Ruler—A large, clear specialty ruler with lots of additional markings. These rulers make it easy to measure seam allowances and stitching lines. To cast your eyes upon one, check out Love It or Leave It: Sewing Tools (page 14).

Raw Edge—An edge of fabric that has been cut or ripped, allowing the threads that create the fabric to unravel over time.

Right Side—The side of your fabric that people will see. This could be the side of your fabric that has a print or a coating. Solid-colored fabrics with no special finish don't technically have a right side; in these instances, you'll need to nominate one side as the right side. Just make sure you note which side you're selecting, as there are subtle differences in the two sides like the direction of the weave, the sheen, or the way the raw edge rolls.

Seam—Where two or more pieces of fabric are sewn together, typically with a straight stitch.

Seam Allowance—The distance between the seam and the edge of your fabric. The raw edge of the seam allowance is finished with a zigzag or overlocking stitch to help hold the seam together and prevent the fabric from fraying. Read all about this in Finishing Seams (page 32).

Seam Ripper—A handheld tool with a sharp metal tip used to unpick stitches. You'll practice using a seam ripper first in Let 'Er Rip (page 35) and then every day you sew for the rest of your life.

Stretch Needle—A special needle designed for sewing knit fabrics. It has a slightly rounded tip that helps prevent it from snagging or ripping knits. I'll give you the lowdown on sewing with knits in The (Fabric) Choice is Yours (page 20).

Top Thread—The spool of thread that sits on the top of the sewing machine. This is the thread that you will thread through your needle and see while you're stitching.

Topstitching—Stitching that will be visible on the right side of a garment. Typically used to secure a hem or seam allowance.

Understitch—A straight stitch along a folded seam allowance to prevent facing or pocket fabric from turning outward.

Walking Foot—A special presser foot used to sew through multiple layers of fabric or bulky/tricky-to-sew fabrics. I personally love to use it for sewing denim, waistbands, and pleather.

Wrong Side—The side of the fabric that people won't see. This is the side of the fabric that is not printed on or does not have a coating. In my case as a thrift-flipper, it often also refers to the side that has stains on it. On solid-colored fabrics, you get to choose which is the right and wrong side.

Zipper Foot—A presser foot used to sew zippers and the edges of fabric. This foot sits directly to the left or right of your needle, allowing your needle to get right up close to a zipper. It's also ideal for sewing in any tight, hard-to-reach places, zipper or no zipper!

Acknowledgments

I would like to acknowledge the Wurundjeri, Wadawurrung, and Bunurong people of the Kulin Nation, the Traditional Owners of the unceded land on which this book was created. Aboriginal people were the first to create and exchange knowledge on this land, and I acknowledge and thank their Elders past and present.

Thank you to so many people:

My parents – for encouraging me through this entire process, reminding me of what I could achieve, and understanding all the weekends I couldn't call because I was writing.

Kirra – for becoming far more than a photographer in this process, but also a friend, cheerleader, and safe space. I'm so glad you complimented my me-made shirt in Lush® that day.

My friends – for always hyping me up and liking, commenting on, and sharing all my Instagram posts when I had no followers.

My dog Louie – for giving me kisses, understanding when I had to write instead of take you for a walk, and being the real star of this book.

Louie's dad – for encouraging me to take on this project when I didn't believe in myself.

My coworkers – for cheering me on and picking up the slack when I was exhausted from late-night writing sessions.

All my incredible English teachers, especially Mrs. Ryan, Mrs. Westmoreland, and Miss Lytton – for making writing a joy.

My Instagram sewing community – for creating a welcoming, encouraging environment to share tips, successes, failures, and overwhelming enthusiasm for this craft.

My followers – for sharing laughter, excitement, struggles, and yourselves with me.

Sadie – for believing in me, being a support system, and making this entire book possible.

The team at Page Street – for your incredible work, pure enthusiasm for publishing, and most importantly, for always being understanding when I was late replying to every email.

About the Author

Allie has been sewing since she was a kid. Her sewing credentials include her popular Instagram account @allie.upcycles, multiple Halloween contest wins, costume designing for summer camp and independent theater productions—and constant reminders from her mom that she's a talented sewist. While Allie is not a formally trained sewist, she has spent years learning, failing, experimenting, and eventually succeeding.

Allie's Instagram account gained popularity for showcasing sewing on an average-sized curvy body, her comedic voice-overs, and her honest approach to sewing and all the good and the bad it brings. Her Instagram account was born from her lifelong passion for arts education. Allie believes that sewing is for absolutely everyone, regardless of shape, size, gender, or previous experience. Her goal is for everyone to learn how to sew so they can hem their own pants instead of constantly asking her.

Index

Note: the following notations indicate the recommended skill level of each project: **(B)** Beginner; **(CB)** Confident Beginner; **(I)** Intermediate; **(A)** Advanced.

A

advanced skill level
    about, 13
    Zipper-ty-Doo-Dah **(A)**, 119–127
All Tied Up **(I)**, 97–104
altering dresses
    adding darts, 53–58
    adding elasticated waistbands, 87–95
    adding seam pockets, 175–181
    adding zippers, 119–127
    attaching external pockets, 167–173
    attaching ties, 97–104
    creating slits, 113–117
    fixing gaping buttons, 109–111
    hemming, 44–47
    letting out seams, 63–66
    taking in seams, 67–72
altering jumpsuits
    adding elasticated waistbands, 87–95
    attaching ties, 97–104
altering pants
    adding darts, 53–58
    adding seam pockets, 175–181
    attaching external pockets, 167–173
    elasticating waistbands, 81–86
    hemming, 44–47
    increasing size by adding fabric, 129–137
    letting out seams, 63–66
    taking in seams, 67–72

altering shirts
    adding darts, 53–58
    adding elasticated waistbands, 87–95
    adding zippers, 119–127
    attaching external pockets, 167–173
    attaching ruffles, 155–163
    attaching ties, 97–104
    creating slits, 113–117
    fixing gaping buttons, 109–111
    hemming, 44–47
    letting out seams, 63–66
    taking in seams, 67–72
altering shorts
    adding darts, 53–58
    adding seam pockets, 175–181
    attaching external pockets, 167–173
    attaching ruffles, 155–163
    creating slits, 113–117
    elasticating waistbands, 81–86
    hemming, 44–47
    increasing size by adding fabric, 129–137
    letting out seams, 63–66
    taking in seams, 67–72
altering skirts
    adding darts, 53–58
    adding seam pockets, 175–181
    adding zippers, 119–127
    attaching external pockets, 167–173
    creating slits, 113–117
    elasticating waistbands, 81–86
    hemming, 44–47
    letting out seams, 63–66
    taking in seams, 67–72
altering tops
    adding darts, 53–58
    adding elasticated waistbands, 87–95

adding zippers, 119–127
attaching external pockets, 167–173
attaching ruffles, 155–163
attaching ties, 97–104
creating slits, 113–117
fixing gaping buttons, 109–111
hemming, 44–47
letting out seams, 63–66
taking in seams, 67–72
applying interfacing to fabrics, 23–24
Around the Bend: Elasticating Tops **(I)**, 87–95
author's profile, 186

B

backstitching, 28
basting, 159
beginner skill level
    about, 12
    altering seams, 63–72
    cropping T-shirts, 73–77
    darts tutorial, 48–52
    fixing gaping buttons, 109–111
    Get This Party Darted **(B)**, 48–52
    Hemming & Hawing **(B)**, 44–47
    ironing straight edges, 42–43
    Let It All Out **(B)**, 63–66
    Let's Crop About It: Cropping T-shirts **(B)**, 73–77
    Let's Get One Thing Straight **(B)**, 40–43
    measuring and marking hems, 45
    measuring and marking straight lines, 40–41
    Mind the (Button) Gap **(B)**, 109–111

seams, altering, 63–72
T-shirts, cropping, 73–77
Take It All In **(B)**, 67–72
belt loops
    reattaching, 86
    seam ripping, 82
bobbins, 14–15
Bring It In: Elasticating Waistbands **(CB)**, 81–86
button-down garments, eliminating gaping, 109–111

C

cap sleeves, replacing, 149–153
Chaco Pen, 16
chalk, 16
changing presser feet, 30–31
clipping corners of seams, 101
confident beginner skill level
    about, 12
    adding darts, 55–58
    attaching external pockets, 167–173
    Bring It In: Elasticating Waistbands **(CB)**, 81–86
    darts, adding, 55–58
    elasticating waistbands, 81–86
    Outsider: External Pockets, The **(CB)**, 167–173
    pockets, attaching externally, 167–173
    Real World: Dart Edition, The **(CB)**, 53–58
    waistbands, elasticating, 81–86
cropping T-shirts, 73–77

D

darts
    about, 48
    in armhole openings, 55–57
    dart legs, 49, 182
    dart points, 49, 182
    dimples, 52
    Get This Party Darted **(B)**, 48–52
    measuring and marking, 49
    in pants waistbands, 55–58

    pinning, 49, 55–56
    pressing, 51, 57
    Real World: Dart Edition, The **(CB)**, 53–58
    sewing, 50
    troubleshooting, 52, 57–58
    tutorials, 48–52, 53–58
    tying off, 50
dimples, dart, 52
dresses
    adding darts, 53–58
    adding elasticated waistbands, 87–95
    adding seam pockets, 175–181
    adding zippers, 119–127
    attaching external pockets, 167–173
    attaching ties, 97–104
    creating slits, 113–117
    fixing gaping buttons, 109–111
    hemming, 44–47
    letting out seams, 63–66
    taking in seams, 67–72

E

edgestitching, 47, 182
elastic
    adding, to dresses and tops, 87–95
    adding, to waistbands, 81–86
    encasing, 90–93
    melting ends of, 83
    types of, 89
encasing elastic in fabric, 90–93
external pockets, attaching, 167–173

F

fabrics
    about, 20–21
    interfacing, 23–24
    knit/stretchy, 20–22, 23, 25
    ribbed, 67
    right side of, 183
    stretchy, 20–22, 25
    woven, 20–21, 32
    wrong side of, 24

facings
    about, 113, 182
    in creating slits, 113–117
    measuring fabric for, 114
    pinning to garments, 115
    sewing to garments, 116–117
"female" garment, 111
finishing seams, 32–34
flat head pins, 17–18
flower head pins, 17, *18*
fraying/unraveling, preventing, 28, 32, 83, 169
fusible interfacing, 23–24

G

gaping button-down garments, fixing, 109–111
gathering, 159–160, 182
Get This Party Darted **(B)**, 48–52
glass head quilting pins, 17
Grow a Pair of Pants **(I)**, 129–137
guiding fabric while sewing, 22
gussets, 141–147

H

hemming cropped T-shirts, 77
Hemming & Hawing **(B)**, 44–47
Hips & Thighs Don't Lie **(I)**, 113–117

I

increasing garment size
    by adding gussets, 141–147
    by combining similar garments, 129–137
    by creating slits, 113–117
    by letting out seams, 63–66
Inside Job: Seam Pockets, The **(I)**, 175–181
interfacing, 23–24, 183
intermediate skill level
    about, 13
    adding elasticated waistbands, 87–95
    adding gussets, 141–147
    adding seam pockets, 175–181

All Tied Up **(I)**, 97–104
Around the Bend: Elasticating Tops **(I)**, 87–95
    creating and attaching ruffles, 155–163
    creating and attaching ties, 97–104
    creating slits, 113–117
    encasing elastic, 90–93
    gathering ruffles, 159–160
    Grow a Pair of Pants **(I)**, 129–137
    gussets, adding, 141–147
    Hips & Thighs Don't Lie **(I)**, 113–117
    increasing size of pants and shorts, 129–137
    Inside Job: Seam Pockets, The **(I)**, 175–181
    loop turning, 101–103
    Replacing C(r)ap Sleeves **(I)**, 149–153
    Ruffling Feathers . . . and Sleeves **(I)**, 155–163
    seam pockets, adding, 175–181
    Side Me Up: Shirt Gussets **(I)**, 141–147
    sleeves, replacing, 149–153
    upsizing pants and shorts, 129–137
    using facing for slits, 113–117
ironing
    along plastic zippers, 127
    altered seams, 66
    darts, 49, 51–52, 57
    hems, 46–47
    interfacing onto fabrics, 23–24
    ruffle seam allowances, 163
    sleeve seams, 153
    straight edges, 42–43
irons/ironing boards, 16

J

jumpsuits
    adding elasticated waistbands, 87–95
    attaching ties, 97–104

K

knit/stretchy fabrics, 20–22, 23, 25

L

lengths of stitches
    about, 25, *27*
    for hemming, 47
    for knit/stretchy fabrics, 22
    for zigzag stitches, *27*, 28
Let It All Out **(B)**, 63–66
Let's Crop About It: Cropping T-shirts **(B)**, 73–77
Let's Get One Thing Straight **(B)**, 40–43
letting out garments, 63–66
lines, marking, 40–41
long stitch lengths, 25, *27*
loop turner/turning, 101–103

M

machines, sewing. *See* sewing machines
"male" garment, 111
markers, washable, 16
marking straight lines, 40–41
matching up and pinning similar garments, 68
measuring tapes, 17
medium stitch lengths, 25, *27*
melting elastic ends, 83
Mind the (Button) Gap **(R)**, 109–111

N

needles, stretch, 21

O

Outsider: External Pockets, The **(CB)**, 167–173
overlockers/overlocking stitch, 33, 183

P

pants
    adding darts, 53–58
    adding seam pockets, 175–181
    attaching external pockets, 167–173
    elasticating waistbands, 81–86
    hemming, 44–47
    increasing size by adding fabric, 129–137
    letting out seams, 63–66
    taking in seams, 67–72
patchwork rulers, 18, 183
pinking shears, 169
pinning
    additional fabric to seams, 134
    anchor fabric to waistbands, 135–136
    belt loops, 86
    darts, 49, 55–56, 58
    elastic encasing fabric, 91
    external pockets, 171–172
    facings, 115
    gussets, 144–146
    hems, 46
    interfacing, 24
    and matching up similar garments, 68
    ruffles, 161
    sleeves to side seams, 152–153
    straight edges, 42–43
    ties to side seams, 103–104
    zippers, 123–125

pins, 17–18, 42
plastic head pins, 17–18
pocket bags, 177, 183
pockets
    external, attaching, 167–173
    seam pockets, 175–181
    waistband darts and, 58
presser feet
    about, 29–30
    changing, 30–31
    standard, 22, 29
    walking feet, 21–22, 29–31, 184
    zipper, 29–30, 110–111, 184
pressing
    along plastic zippers, 127
    altered seams, 66
    darts, 49, 51–52, 57
    hems, 46–47
    interfacing onto fabrics, 23–24
    ruffle seam allowances, 163
    sleeve seams, 153
    straight edges, 42–43
profile of author, 186
projects by name
    All Tied Up (I), 97–104
    Around the Bend: Elasticating Tops (I), 87–95
    Bring It In: Elasticating Waistbands (CB), 81–86
    Get This Party Darted (B), 48–52
    Grow a Pair of Pants (I), 129–137
    Hemming & Hawing (B), 44–47
    Inside Job: Seam Pockets, The (I), 175–181
    Let It All Out (B), 63–66
    Let's Crop About It: Cropping T-shirts (B), 73–77
    Let's Get One Thing Straight (B), 40–43
    Mind the (Button) Gap (B), 109–111
    Outsider: External Pockets, The (CB), 167–173
    Real World: Dart Edition, The (CB), 53–58
    Replacing C(r)ap Sleeves (I), 149–153
    Ruffling Feathers . . . and Sleeves (I), 155–163
    Side Me Up: Shirt Gussets (I), 141–147
    Take It All In (B), 67–72
    Zipper-ty-Doo-Dah (A), 119–127

Q
quilting pins, 17
quilting rulers, 18, 183

R
raw edges
    about, 20, 32
    concealing, with facing, 113–117, 182
    finishing, 33–34
Real World: Dart Edition, The (CB), 53–58
reducing garment size
    by elasticating waistbands, 81–86
    by taking in seams, 67–72
    Replacing C(r)ap Sleeves (I), 149–153
ribbed fabric, sewing, 67
rippers, seam, 18–19
ripping seams
    about, 35
    of belt loops, 82
    of cap sleeves, 150–151
    of hems, 36, 65, 70
    inside-the-seam method, 37–38
    outside-of-the-seam method, 36
    overlocked seams, 38–39
    of sleeves, 150–151
    of waistbands, 131–132
Ruffling Feathers . . . and Sleeves (I), 155–163
rulers, 18, 183

S
scissors for sewing, 19, 169
seam allowances
    about, 183
    finishing, 32–34
    in hems, 70–71
    for letting out garments, 63–64
seam rippers, 18–19
seam ripping
    about, 35
    belt loops, 82
    cap sleeves, 150–151
    hems, 36, 65, 70
    inside-the-seam method, 37–38
    outside-of-the-seam method, 36
    overlocked seams, 38–39
    sleeves, 150–151
    waistbands, 131–132
seams
    clipping corners of, 101
    finishing, 32–34
    in knit/stretchy fabrics, 22–23
    unfinished, 32
sergers, 33
sewing machines
    about, 19
    bobbins, 14–15
    needles, 21
    overlockers, 33
    presser feet, 21–22, 29–31, 110–111, 183–184
    sergers, 33
    stitch lengths, 22, 25, 27
    stitch types, 27–28
    stretch needles, 21
    walking feet, 21–22, 29–31, 184
    zipper feet, 29–30, 110–111
sewing scissors, 19, 169
sewing skill levels, 12–13
sewing tools
    bobbins, 14–15
    Chaco Pen, 16
    chalk, 16
    irons/ironing boards, 16
    measuring tape, 17

pinking shears, 169
pins, 17–18
rulers, 18, 183
scissors, 19, 169
seam rippers, 18–19
sewing machines, 19, 33
teacher's chalk, 16
thread, 14–15, 19, 183
washable markers, 16
shirts
    adding darts, 53–58
    adding elasticated waistbands, 87–95
    adding zippers, 119–127
    attaching external pockets, 167–173
    attaching ruffles, 155–163
    attaching ties, 97–104
    creating slits, 113–117
    fixing gaping buttons, 109–111
    hemming, 44–47
    letting out seams, 63–66
    taking in seams, 67–72
short stitch lengths, 22, 25, *27*
shortening T-shirts, 73–77
shorts
    adding darts, 53–58
    adding seam pockets, 175–181
    attaching external pockets, 167–173
    attaching ruffles, 155–163
    creating slits, 113–117
    elasticating waistbands, 81–86
    hemming, 44–47
    increasing size by adding fabric, 129–137
    letting out seams, 63–66
    taking in seams, 67–72
Side Me Up: Shirt Gussets **(I)**, 141–147
skill levels, 12–13
skirts
    adding darts, 53–58
    adding seam pockets, 175–181
    adding zippers, 119–127
    attaching external pockets, 167–173
    creating slits, 113–117
    elasticating waistbands, 81–86

hemming, 44–47
letting out seams, 63–66
taking in seams, 67–72
slacks. *See* pants
sleeves
    adding gussets to, 141–147
    attaching external pockets, 167–173
    attaching ruffles, 155–163
    replacing, 149–153
    seam ripping, 150–151
slits, 113–117
spool pin, 15
standard presser feet, 22, 29
step-by-step tutorials. *See* tutorials
stitch lengths
    about, 25, *27*
    for hemming, 47
    for knit/stretchy fabrics, 22
    for zigzag stitches, *27*, 28
stitch types
    about, 27
    backstitch, 28
    basting, 159, 182
    edgestitch, 47, 182
    overlock, 33–34, 183
    straight, 27
    topstitch, 136, 183
    understitch, 179
    zigzag, 27–28, 34
straight edges, ironing, 42–43
straight lines, marking, 40–41
straight stitch, 27
stretch needles, 21
stretchy fabrics, 20–22, 23, 25

T
T-shirts, cropping, 73–77
tailor's chalk, 16
tailor's ham, 51
Take It All In **(B)**, 67–72
teacher's chalk, 16
thread
    about, 19
    bobbin thread, 14–15
    thread holder, 15
    top thread, 14–15, 183
    winding bobbins, 15

threading elastic, 82–85, 92–94
ties
    attaching to garments, 103–104
    cutting fabric for, 99–100
    determining measurements of, 98–100
    loop turning, 101–103
    sewing fabric for, 100–101
tools for sewing
    bobbins, 14–15
    Chaco Pen, 16
    chalk, 16
    irons/ironing boards, 16
    measuring tape, 17
    pins, 17–18
    rulers, 18, 183
    scissors, 19, 169
    seam rippers, 18–19
    sewing machines, 19, 33
    sewing scissors, 19
    teacher's chalk, 16
    thread, 14–15, 19, 183
    washable markers, 16
top thread, 14, 183
tops
    adding darts, 53–58
    adding elasticated waistbands, 87–95
    adding zippers, 119–127
    attaching external pockets, 167–173
    attaching ruffles, 155–163
    attaching ties, 97–104
    creating slits, 113–117
    fixing gaping buttons, 109–111
    hemming, 44–47
    letting out seams, 63–66
    taking in seams, 67–72
topstitching, 183
trousers. *See* pants
tutorials
    adding zippers, 119–127
    All Tied Up **(I)**, 97–104
    applying interfacing to fabrics, 24
    Around the Bend: Elasticating Tops **(I)**, 87–95
    attaching ruffles, 155–163
    bobbin threading, 15

Bring It In: Elasticating Waistbands **(CB)**, 81–86
creating darts, 48–58
creating slits, 113–117
Get This Party Darted **(B)**, 48–52
Grow a Pair of Pants **(I)**, 129–137
gussets, adding, 141–147
Hemming & Hawing **(B)**, 44–47
Hips & Thighs Don't Lie **(I)**, 113–117
Inside Job: Seam Pockets, The **(I)**, 175–181
ironing straight edges, 42–43
Let It All Out **(B)**, 63–66
Let's Crop About It: Cropping T-shirts **(B)**, 73–77
Let's Get One Thing Straight **(B)**, 40–43
marking straight lines, 40–41
Mind the (Button) Gap **(B)**, 109–111
Outsider: External Pockets, The **(CB)**, 167–173
pockets, adding, 167–173
Real World: Dart Edition, The **(CB)**, 53–58
Replacing C(r)ap Sleeves **(I)**, 149–153
Ruffling Feathers . . . and Sleeves **(I)**, 155–163
Side Me Up: Shirt Gussets **(I)**, 141–147
sleeves, replacing, 149–153
Take It All In **(B)**, 67–72
threading bobbins, 15
Zipper-ty-Doo-Dah **(A)**, 119–127
tying off darts, 50

U
understitching, 179
unfinished seams, 32
unraveling/fraying, preventing, 28, 32, 83, 169
upsizing garments
    about, 107
    by combining similar garments, 129–137
    by creating slits, 113–117
    by fixing gaping buttons, 109–111
    by letting out seams, 63–66

W
waistbands
    adding darts to, 55–58
    elasticating, 81–86
    seam ripping, 131–132
walking feet, 21–22, 29–31, 184
washable markers, 16
winding bobbins, 15
woven fabrics, 20–21, 32
wrong side of fabrics, 24

Z
zigzag stitch, 27–28, 34
zipper feet, 29–30, 110–111
Zipper-ty-Doo-Dah **(A)**, 119–127
zippers
    plastic, ironing along, 127
    selecting proper length, 122
    sewing into garment, 122–125, 127
    shortening, 126